Top 25 locator map
(continues on inside
back cover)
◄

CityPack
Montréal

TIM JEPSON

If you have any comments
or suggestions for this guide
you can contact the editor at
Citypack@theAA.com

AA Publishing
Find out more about AA Publishing and the
wide range of services the AA provides by
visiting our website at *www.theAA.com*

About This Book

KEY TO SYMBOLS

✚ Map reference to the accompanying fold-out map, and Top 25 locator map

✉ Address

☎ Telephone number

🕐 Opening/closing times

🍴 Restaurant or café on premises or nearby

🚆 Nearest railway station

🚌 Nearest bus route

⛴ Nearest riverboat or ferry stop

♿ Facilities for visitors with disabilities

✋ Admission charges: Inexpensive ($5 or less), Moderate ($6–10), and Expensive (over $10)

↔ Other nearby places of interest

❓ Other practical information

➤ Indicates the page where you will find a fuller description

ℹ Tourist information

ORGANIZATION

This guide is divided into six chapters:

- Planning Ahead, Getting There
- Living Montréal—Montréal Now, Montréal Then, Time to Shop, Out and About, Walks, Montréal by Night
- Montréal's Top 25 Sights
- Montréal's Best—best of the rest
- Where To—detailed listings of restaurants, hotels, shops, and nightlife
- Travel Facts—practical information

The colours of the tabs on the page corners match the colours of the triangles aligned with the chapter names on the contents page opposite.

MAPS

The fold-out map in the wallet at the back of this book is a comprehensive street plan of Montréal. The first (or only) grid reference given for each attraction refers to this map. **The Top 25 locator map** found on the inside front and back covers of the book itself is for quick reference. It shows the Top 25 Sights, described on pages 26–50, which are clearly plotted by number (**1** –**25**, not page number) across the city. The second map reference given for the Top 25 Sights refers to this map.

Contents

Planning Ahead

WHEN TO GO

The best time to visit Montréal is between late May and late October. The summer from the end of June to the first weekend in September is rich in festivals. Later in the autumn the weather is cooler and better for walking; the countryside can be spectacular. In winter, a visit can be coupled with a trip to a ski resort.

TIME

Montréal operates on Eastern Standard Time, 3 hours ahead of Los Angeles, 5 hours behind London.

AVERAGE MAXIMUM DAILY TEMPERATURES

	JAN	FEB	MAR	APR	MAY	JUN	JUL	AUG	SEP	OCT	NOV	DEC
°F	18°F	20°F	31°F	45°F	63°F	73°F	79°F	77°F	69°F	56°F	43°F	33°F
°C	-8°C	-7°C	-1°C	7°C	17°C	23°C	26°C	25°C	21°C	13°C	6°C	1°C

Spring (April to May) The leap between winter and summer can be very abrupt. It is also the least attractive time of year as the melting snow reveals dead grass littered with the debris of winter. **Summer** (June to August) begins on 24 June, the date of Québec Fête National. The city can be very hot and humid, especially in downtown.
Autumn (September to October), with cooler temperatures and sunny days, makes for ideal exploring. There are fewer visitors, so you can see the city as the locals do. **Winter** (November to March), Montréal's defining season, can be brutally cold with occasional blizzards that shut down the city. There's often a brief thaw in January.

WHAT'S ON

January/February *Fête des Neiges:* Ice and snow celebrations on Îles Notre-Dame and Sainte-Hélène.
March *St. Patrick's Day Parade:* North America's third largest.
April–September Baseball season for the Montréal Expos.
May *Festival de Théâtre des Ameriques:* New drama.
June *Festival du Nouveau Cinéma:* Independent and avant-garde films/videos. *International Fireworks Competition:* Pyrotechnics on Thursdays and Sundays

(mid-June to mid-July). *Grand Prix du Canada:* Formula 1 racing on Île Notre-Dame. *Tour d'Île:* 40,000 cyclists attempt this 66km (41mi) trek through the city streets. *Fête Vieux-Port:* Concerts, dancing, and other entertainment through the first Monday in September. *Mozart Plus:* Montréal Symphony Orchestra concerts in Basilique Notre-Dame.
July *International Jazz Festival:* Largest celebration of jazz in the world.

Juste Pour Rire: The world's largest comedy festival. *Nuits d'Afrique:* Traditional African music and festivities on boulevard Saint-Laurent. *Franco Folies:* 1,000 musicians in a celebration of French songs and music.
August *Omnium du Maurier:* International tennis. *Les Fêtes Gourmandes Internationales de Montréal:* Outdoor festival where you can sample world foods. *Festival des Films du Monde:* World film festival.
September–May *L'Opéra de Montréal:* The opera season.

MONTRÉAL ONLINE

www.montrealplus.ca
This broad travel guide provides information about Montréal lodging, dining, shopping, and entertainment.

www.old.montreal.qc.ca
A comprehensive guide to historic Vieux-Montréal. Includes live web cams, maps, and historical information and tours.

www.canada.com/montreal
News and features from the Montréal Gazette, the city's daily newspaper.

www.tourisme-montreal.org
You can download maps, print out itineraries, and read up on attractions and coming events on this, the official tourist information website for Montréal.

www.montrealjazzfest.com
Every year some 2,000 big-name jazz musicians perform more than 500 shows in Montréal's largest festival, the Festival International de Jazz de Montréal. This site includes a venue map, ticket information, and performer news.

www.hahaha.com
The Just for Laughs comedy festival propelled performers such as Jerry Seinfeld and Ray Romano to comedy superstardom. This site has the latest news on who's coming to this year's festival and ticket information.

www.pdi-montreal.com
The site of Expo 67, Park Jean-Drapeau is an island jewel surrounded by the Saint Lawrence River. You can browse for information on tourist attractions, events, services, maps, and history.

www.menumontreal.com
With more than 5,000 eateries, Montréal is arguably the restaurant capital of Canada. You can narrow your search for the perfect meal by keyword or district on this funky restaurant site.

GOOD TRAVEL SITES

www.fodors.com
A complete travel-planning site. You can research prices and weather; book air tickets, cars and rooms; ask questions (and get answers) from fellow travellers; and find links to other sites.

www.montreal.com
Exhaustive lists of what to do, and where to sleep and eat. You'll find information for all tastes from tourist sights to local activities.

CYBERCAFÉS

Café Internet
12 PCs. Coffee and sandwiches.
✚ E8 ✉ 1425 rue Mackay ☎ 514/287-9100
🕐 Mon–Fri 10–10; Sun 12–8

Atwater Library and Computer Centre
A centre with eight PCs and one Mac. No food.
✚ E9 ✉ 120 avenue Atwater ☎ 514/935-7344
🕐 Mon, Wed 9–7; Sat 10–6; Sun 12–6
✋ $4 per hour.

Getting There

US citizens need two items of proof of US permanent residency (driver's licence and birth certificate). Otherwise a passport is necessary. Citizens of the EU and of most British Commonwealth countries need a passport but no visa.

MONEY

US dollars are widely accepted but for the best exchange rate take your currency to a bank or currency exchange office. ATM cards are widely accepted. French speakers sometimes call a penny a "sou," the nickel "cinq sous," and the quarter "vingt-cinq sous." English speakers call the dollar coin "looney" after the bird (a loon) on its obverse. They call the bimetal $2 coin a "tooney."

10 Dollars

20 Dollars

50 Dollars

ARRIVING

Montréal has two airports. Aéroport de Dorval is 22.5km (14mi) southwest of the city and handles commercial flights; Aéroport de Mirabel is 56km (35mi) northwest of the city and handles charter flights.

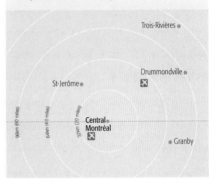

FROM AÉROPORT DE DORVAL

For airport information ☎ 514/394-7377. A taxi to downtown takes 25 minutes in light traffic and costs $28. Aérobus (☎ 514/921-9002) operates a shuttle every 30 minutes 5AM–11PM in front of the terminal building to the Station Centrale Berri, with stops at the Hotel Marriott Château Champlain, the Station Aérobus at 777 rue de la Gauchetière Ouest, and the Hôtel Le Reine Elizabeth. The fare is $11. Aérobus operates a shuttle service to Aéroport de Mirabel.

FROM AÉROPORT DE MIRABEL

For airport information ☎ 514/394-7377. A taxi to downtown takes about an hour and the meter-determined fare runs to $60–65. Aérobus shuttles (☎ 514/921-9002) leave from in front of the terminal building for the 5-minute ride to the Gare Centrale Berri, stopping at the Hôtel Marriott Château Champlain, the Station Aérobus at 777 rue de la Gauchetière Ouest, and the Hôtel Le Reine Elizabeth. Service varies from four trips on Thursday to 21 on Sunday. The fare is $20. Aérobus operates a shuttle service to the Aéroport de Dorval.

Arriving by Train

Trains run by Amtrak (☎ 800/USA-RAIL) and Canadian VIA Rail (☎ 514/871-9395 or 800/361-5390 in Québec province) arrive at the Gare Centrale, 895 rue de la Gauchetière Ouest.

Arriving by Bus

Montréal's bus terminal is the Station Centrale Berri (✉ 514/842-2281). It handles all bus services from Montréal and its phone system has information about bus companies serving all destinations including Greyhound (for American and Canadian destinations), Adirdondack Trailways (New York), Voyageur (Ontario), and Orléans Express (Quebec City), as well as the companies that service Quebec's smaller communities. The journey takes 8.5 hours to New York, 3 hours to Québec City, and 6.5 hours to Toronto.

Getting Around

Montréal has more than 150 bus routes and a Métro system with 65 stations and links to more than 20 miles (32km) of walkways in the Underground City (✉ 514/288-6287; www.stcum.qc.ca). There are four colour-coded lines (green, orange, blue, and yellow) their direction is indicated by the name of their terminus. You can buy flat-fare one-way tickets, either as singles or in a discounted strip called a *carnet* at Métro booths and some retail outlets, but not on buses. Tickets are good on both the Métro and the buses, but if you have to change from one to the other, get a transfer (*correspondence* in French) from your bus driver or from the machine in the Métro station where your journey started. Weekly and monthly passes are available. Bus passengers with no ticket, pass, or transfer must have the exact fare.

The orange, green, and yellow lines operate Monday to Friday 5.30AM–1AM; Saturday 5.30AM–1.30AM; Sunday 5.30AM–2AM. The blue line runs daily between 5.30AM–11PM. Most buses run until around 12.30AM, when a night service takes over on 27 routes.

Taxis stand outside main hotels, near the railway station, and at major intersections, and can be hailed on the street.

INSURANCE

Travel insurance, including coverage for medical costs, is strongly recommended. Check your insurance coverage and buy a supplementary policy as needed.

VISITORS WITH DISABILITIES

Montréal's Métro system is not adapted for wheelchairs. There are no lifts and the escalators are not always dependable, so deep stations such as Snowdon and Lucien-L'Allier are difficult for anyone with mobility diffculties. The new, low-slung buses are a little better. Passengers with a cane or crutches can embark with care. They also accept wheelchairs at the rear exit doors, but space is limited and the entrance tight. Most major attractions and hotels are much better with ramps and lifts, and facilities to help hearing- and vision-impaired visitors. For additional information contact Kéroul, 4545 avenue Pierre-De Coubertin, Box 1000, Branch M, Montréal, H1V 3R (☎ 514/252-3104; infos@keroul.qc.ca; www.kitweb.com/kw/keroul/).

Living
Montréal

Montréal Now

Above: *Old Viger Station among the high-rise towers of downtown Montréal*

Give Montréalers just the ghost of a theme and they'll turn it into a party. Which is why the world's biggest jazz festival is held on an island in the St. Lawrence River and not on the shores of the Mississippi, and why the biggest comedy festival (Juste Pour Rire) is bilingual. But jazz and jokes are easy—those festivals are in summer. If you really want to see how the city works come in February, when the nights are long, the days are cold, and Montréal

---

LOCAL PARLANCE

• Montréal's English has not escaped the French influence. For example, many English-speaking residents don't turn lights off and on, they open and shut them—this is a literal translation of the French. When an anglophone runs out of bread or needs a case of beer, he heads for a *dépanneur*, not a convenience store. And nearly all Montréalers send their children to junior colleges called CÉGEPs (pronounced "say-jeps" by francophones and "see-jeps" by anglophones. Very few of either group know that it stands for College d'Éducation Generale et Professionelle.

Above: *sailing past the Casino de Montréal*
Centre and left: *calm and colour in the Jardin Botanique de Montréal*

BALCONVILLE

● Many Montréalers live in duplexes and triplexes, stacked residences built in the 1930s and 1940s to house the city's blue-collar workers. Curving, wrought-iron staircases link the balconies of the various levels, a building strategy that saved interior space and inadvertently created pleasing places to gather round in the summer.

en Lumière (the Montréal Highlights Festival) is in full swing. Invented simply to brighten winter's deadest month, the festival is an odd mix of illuminated buildings, jazz, and classical concerts, with guest appearances by visiting chefs. It's doubtful such an hodgepodge would fly in any other Canadian city, but in Montréal it has locals and a growing number of winter visitors eating, humming, and tromping about the snow oohing at artily lighted buildings.

Montréal is irrepressible. Nothing seems capable of dampening its spirit—not uncertain politics, not linguistic squabbles, and certainly not hard winters. Canada's second-largest city—

The Tour de Montréal curves
up above the Biodôme

PRINTED PAGE

• Mordecai Richler
brings the vibrant,
hard-scrabble life of
Montréal's Jewish
community to life in the
classic *St. Urban's
Horseman* and The
*Apprenticeship of
Duddy Kravitz* (made
into a film starring
Richard Dreyfuss).
Gabrielle Roy captured
the struggles of the
French-speaking
population in *Bonheur
d'Occasion* (translated
as *The Tin Flute*).

and the continent's only French-speaking
metropolis—is no longer the great financial
centre it was in the late 19th century but it still
has flair. Toronto's stockbrokers might be richer
but they don't dress nearly as snappily as
Montréal's, and they probably don't dance
as well either.

A lot of people credit this sense of urban style to
Latin exuberance, but that's nonsense.
Montréal's French speakers are largely
descended from hard-headed Normans, not
loquacious Mediterranean types from Provence.
And the city's English speakers are by and large
Celts. No, the spirit is homegrown, with lots of
help from the immigrants who flooded into the
city in the last 200 years—Italians, Greeks,
Germans, Portuguese, Spaniards, Guatemalans,
Africans, Romanians, Haitians and Jamaicans,
Lebanese, and Asians from India, Pakistan, and
Vietnam—along with a sprinkling of Americans
fleeing revolution, conscription, and slavery at
home.

What this has produced is a city with four universities (two English, two French), a vibrant

entertainment industry that functions in two languages, a fashion hothouse that makes every other city in the country look dowdy, and a population that will sit in bars and coffee shops until all hours arguing, often in several languages at the same time, about anything.

The 1912 concourse at Windsor Station still welcomes the modern traveller

NEIGHBOURHOODS

• Montréal is an agglomeration of neighbourhoods and communities. **Vieux-Montréal** is a waterfront area that corresponds closely to the walled city of the French colonial period. Most buildings on its cobbled street date from the 19th century. **The Square Mile** is where powerful men once controlled most of Canada's wealth from mansions on the slopes of Mont-Royal. Today the district includes much of downtown, many of the city's leading museums, and the campus of McGill University. Francophone and immigrant blue-collar workers' families share the charming **Plateau Mont-Royal** with a growing number of students, academics, and young professionals. The area abounds with boutiques, clubs, and restaurants in all price ranges. Visitors come to **Quartier Latin** for its cinemas, theatres, outdoor cafés, and the Carré Saint-Louis.

FAMOUS MONTRÉALERS

• Montréal's famous include *Star Trek's* William Shatner, jazz great Oscar Peterson, novelist Mordecai Richler, film director Denys Arcand, theatre director Robert Lepage, and poet-singer Leonard Cohen. Confederate president Jefferson Davis lived in the city briefly after the American Civil War and singer Céline Dion was born in Repentigny.

13

Above: *Balconville, a classy style of duplex architecture*
Above right: *the Musée d'art contemporain*
Centre: *Juste Pour Rire, Montréal's famous comedy festival*

That's not to say, however, that Montréal is all glitz and no substance, and that food, fashion, and entertainment are the only things that keep it afloat. It's still an important port with links both to the Great Lakes and the Atlantic. The city has a long and solid history with plenty of cobbled streets and soaring churches to remind you of its proud past. And its glittering ranks of glass-and-steel skyscrapers are full of young entrepreneurs who have made a name for themselves in such diverse fields as

MONTRÉAL ON FILM

• Montréal has been in a lot of films, but seldom plays itself. One recent exception is the 2001 film *The Score*, with Robert de Niro (who even spoke a little French) and Marlon Brando. For a completely different look at Montréal, try Denys Arcand's *Jésus de Montréal* (it comes with English subtitles).

communications technology, pharmaceuticals, transportation, as well as aircraft design.

Above: *a bug's eye view— the Insectarium in the Jardin Botanique*

No city is perfect and Montréal has its share of problems too. There's the harsh winter. And then there's the language thing that hovers around the edges: anglophones distraught at seeing their language banned by law from public display; francophones worried that their language will disappear in North America's vast English sea; and puzzled allophones (that's the official term for everyone else) wondering what the fuss is all about.

When all is said and done, the most striking things about Montréal are its sense of fun and style, its wit and sparkle, and its grace under the most serious political and climactic pressure. "Joie de vivre" is a tiresome cliché much indulged in by visiting travel writers—but here it fits.

CHANGE OF DIRECTION

● Montréalers determine east and west by the flow of the St. Lawrence River, which actually flows southwest to northeast as it swirls around the island. What everyone calls the East End and the West End are closer to being the south end and the north end.

15

Montréal Then

EARLY DAYS

In 1535 French explorer Jacques Cartier became the first European to set foot in the native village of Hochelaga, the site of modern-day Montréal. He named the hill above the village Mont-Royal—this was translated to Mont-Real by Italian writer G. B. Ramuso in 1556.

FUR CONFLICTS

Montréal was the staging ground of the only Confederate raid on New England during the Civil War in the United States. On 19 October 1864, 20 cavalrymen swooped down on St. Albans, Vermont. The raiders robbed three banks and made off with more than $200,000 before the stunned Vermonters could react. The raiders were arrested in Montréal.

1642 Paul de Chomedey, a French soldier, establishes Ville-Marie on the island of Montréal. He is helped by Jeanne Mance.

1663 King Louis XIV gives land rights on Île de Mont-Real to the Sulpicians, a religious order trying to convert the native population, aided by vision-seeing Marguerite de Bourgeoys.

1682 Ville-Marie becomes HQ of the Compagnie du Nord, fur-trading rivals of the Hudson's Bay Company.

1701 The French sign a treaty with the native Iroquois, ending over 50 years of conflict following the Iroquois massacre of the Hurons, allies of the French, in 1649.

1710 The name Ville-Marie is dropped.

1754 The French and Indian War breaks out between England and France. In 1759 General James Wolfe is mortally wounded during the capture of French Quebec and in 1760 the British take Montréal. The 1763 Treaty of Paris ends the war and cedes Canada to Britain.

1775 American revolutionary troops occupy Montréal in an effort to enlist French Canadians to their cause.

1832 Montréal is North America's second largest city.

1844 Montréal becomes the capital of the new United Province of Canada.

1867 The Dominion of Canada is formed, consisting of Québec, Ontario, New Brunswick, and Nova Scotia.

1874 Parc Mont Royal is laid out by Frederick Law Olmstead.

1940 Colourful mayor Camillien Houde is interned after urging Canadians not to register for wartime conscription.

1959 The St. Lawrence Seaway opens.

1969 Canada's federal government recognizes both French and English as official languages.

1970 Nationalist terrorists kidnap a provincial cabinet minister and a British diplomat, triggering one of Canada's worst political crises. Quebec government makes French the province's only official language.

1995 Barely 50 percent of Québécois vote to remain part of Canada.

2002 All 24 municipalities on the Island of Montréal merge into one super city.

Left to right: Jacques Cartier lands in the New World; the Huron massacre in 1649; General James Wolfe lies fatally wounded during the French and Indian War; the St. Lawrence Seaway; Expo '67—the Biosphère

ACHIEVEMENTS

● The opening of the Lachine Canal in 1825 allows ships to travel between the Atlantic and the Great Lakes.

● The completion of the Canadian Pacific Railway in 1886 links Montréal to the Pacific coast, helping the city to develop into the financial and industrial capital of Canada.

● Montréal's Expo '67 world fair, celebrating Canada's centennial, attracts 53 million visitors.

● Montréal hosts the summer Olympic Games in 1976.

Time to Shop

Le shopping—now there's a word that crosses linguistic boundaries. Some Québécois may still *magasinent*, but the truly stylish *font le shopping*. And Montréal is nothing if not stylish. The women dress well and, more tellingly, so do the men. Montréal is Canada's fashion capital, with a

TASTEFUL SOUVENIRS

Try such local delicacies as smoked meat and bagels (Montréal's are lighter and crisper than the New York version). Local markets stock a wide variety of Québec cheeses—bries, chèvres, and sharp cheddars. Some of the finest are made by the Benedictine monks of Saint Benoît de Lac. Trappist colleagues in the Lac Saint-Jean region make one of the city's favourite sweet treats: chocolate-covered blueberries. They arrive in late summer and vanish almost immediately. For something meatier look for jars of Canards Lac-Brome pâtés and confit, as well as packages of smoked duck breast. And if you're looking for a sweet gift pick up some maple sugar.

clothing industry that employs 72,000 people. Five fashion schools churn out talent to challenge the leadership Léo Chevalier, Michel Robichaud, and John Warden. And if you're looking for children's clothes, this is the place. Houses like Petits Poids, La Mère Michel, and Souris Mini keep the younger set looking good. Shoppers can find all the best stuff in the city's boutiques and department stores, but the bargain hunter seeks out the little factories that sell goods to the public on Saturday mornings. The fashion passion extends beyond clothes to jewellery, fragrances, handbags, shoes, and other essential accessories.

In the same vein—but less politically correct—is the fur industry. Trade in animal skins made the city wealthy in the first place, and given the city's climate, it's not surprising that furs are still popular winter wear. However, some designers have taken a less traditional approach to cold-weather wear. The multilayered winter wear of

Kanuk is stylish and comfortable. More sporty and certainly more colourful are the winter clothes from Chlorophylle.

Montréal's age makes it a mecca for antiques collectors. Dozens of shops in Westmount,

Below: antiques shops on boulevard Saint-Laurent and rue Notre-Dame

along the west end of rue Notre-Dame and in the Gay Village cater to just about every taste, with furniture from colonial Québec to 1950s retro. Keep an eye out for rare books in both languages, as well as Victorian paintings, religious articles and decorations, china, and silverware. Many shops also stock English and European antiques.

Québec's artistic traditions reach back to the days of New France, when the colony's Catholic bishops kept dozens of artists hard at work, decorating churches with mosaics, paintings, sculptures, and stained glass. Dozens of galleries service more modern tastes with work by leading local artists like Paul Fenniak, Betty Goodwin, and Jean-Louis Èmond. If your tastes lean more to the traditional, consider a startlingly realistic wood carving by a Québec folk artist or a graceful soapstone sculpture by one of Canada's Inuit carvers.

A GOOD SMOKE

Canada has never severed diplomatic or trade relations with Cuba, and so just about every tobacconist in Montréal has a humidor full of Havanas—something you won't find anywhere south of the US border. But be careful: US laws embargo trade with Cuba and trying to take goods across the border could lead to charges. Visitors from elsewhere, however, can take a handsome Montecristo home if they so wish.

19

Out and About

GUIDED TOURS

Gray Line
Nine different Montréal coach tours in summer.
✉ Tickets: Infotouriste, 1001 Square-Dorchester
☎ 514/934-1222

Autocar Royal
City tours in a trolley bus.
✉ Tickets: Infotouriste, 1001 Square-Dorchester
☎ 514/871-4733

Amphi-Bus
Tours the streets then takes to the water.
✉ Rue de la Commune at boulevard Saint-Laurent
☎ 514/849-5181

Vélo-Tour Montréal
Bicycle tours.
✉ 99 rue de la Commune Ouest
☎ 514/847-0666

Guidatour
Guided walks of Vieux-Montréal.
✉ 477 Saint-François-Xavier
☎ 514/844-4021

INFORMATION

Musée Ferroviaire
Distance 19km (12mi) south
Journey Time 20–30 minutes
✉ 122a rue Saint-Pierre, Saint Constant
☎ 450/632-2410
🕐 May–Oct: daily 9–5. Sep–Oct: Sat, Sun
Ⓜ Longueuil and Angrignon, then bus

ORGANIZED SIGHTSEEING

Various bus, bicycle, and walking tours are available in Montréal. You can also choose a specialized tour, such as the one run by Tours Maisonneuve (☎ 514/256-4636), which visits places associated with famous Montréalers.

For trips further afield, Orléans Express (☎ 514/842-2281) and Gray Line (☎ 514/934-1222) offer excursions to Quebec City, the hills of the Laurentians, and the vineyards of the Eastern Townships. Particularly popular are autumn foliage tours and trips to the Roman Catholic shrine in Sainte-Anne-de-Beaupré. Croisières Navimex (☎ 514/849-9136) offers voyages to Quebec City.

EXCURSIONS
Musée Ferroviaire Canadien

If you have even a passing interest in trains and railways, visit the Musée Ferroviaire Canadien (Canadian Railway Museum, above), one of North America's largest collections of steam engines and railroad memorabilia. On the 6ha (15-acre) site are trams, boxcars, steam engines, cabooses, diners, diesels, trolleybuses, snow ploughs, and even horse-drawn sleighs. Among the engines and train cars on show are CPR 5935, one of the largest locomotives ever built, and BR 60010, which once hauled the *Flying Scotsman* in Britain. Trams and steam engines can usually be seen working on Sundays.

LACHINE

Lachine, on the southern edge of Montréal, makes an interesting break from downtown. The best known of its sights is the Lieu Historique National du Commerce-de-la-Fourrure (Fur Trade National Historic Site), a restored stone

trading post built for the Hudson's Bay Company in 1803. Close by is the Centre d'Interprétation du Canal de Lachine, a centre devoted to the Lachine Canal. The Musée de la Ville (above), a museum of pioneer memorabilia, is housed in one of Montréal's oldest buildings.

OKA AND HUDSON

English-speaking Hudson provides a charming riverside escape from the city. Its pretty streets are ideal for strolling and you can browse among its antiques shops. On summer Saturdays the town hosts Finnegan's Market (Main Street), the largest antiques and flea market in Quebec. A 10-minute ferry ride across the Ottawa River takes you to the orchard-covered hills of Oka, a pretty village whose tranquillity was marred in 1990 by a summer-long stand off between the army and Mohawk natives, angry at plans to build a golf course on an ancient burial site. Pilgrims come here every year to make the Stations of the Cross at the Calvaire d'Oka, a commemoration of Christ's passion and death, built by Sulpician priests in 1739. Another holy site is the Cistercian abbey founded by French monks in 1880.

INFORMATION

LACHINE
Distance 10km (6mi)
Journey Time 15 minutes
🚇 Angrignon
🚌 195 Ouest for Historic Site and Interpretative Centre; 110 for Museum
Historic Site
✉ 1255 boulevard Saint-Joseph, Lachine
☎ 514/637-7433
🕐 Apr to mid-Oct: Mon 1–6; Tue–Sun 10–12.30, 1–6. Mid-Oct to early Dec: Wed–Sun 9.30–12.30, 1–5
Interpretative Centre
✉ Boulevard Saint-Joseph at 7ième Avenue
☎ 514/637-7433
🕐 Mid-May to early Sep: Mon 1–6; Tue–Sun 10–12, 1–6
Museum
✉ 110 chemin LaSalle (10km (6mi) south)
☎ 514/634-3471
🕐 Apr to mid-Dec: Wed–Sun 11.30–4.30

INFORMATION

OKA AND HUDSON
Distance 20km (13mi) west
Journey Time 25 minutes
✉ Abbey: 1600 chemin d'Oka, Oka
🕐 Abbey Mon–Fri 9.30–11.30, 1–5; Sat 9–5. Finnegan's Market May–late Oct: Sat
☎ Abbey: 450/458-4377
🚉 Gare Windsor to Hudson, then ferry to Oka

Walks

INFORMATION

Distance 3km (2mi)
Time 2–6 hours, depending on sights visited
Start point
★ Place Jacques-Cartier
🔲 G7
🚇 Champ-de-Mars
🚌 7
End point Place Jacques-Cartier
🕐 Most sights are open all day
🍴 Vieux-Montréal is well provided with cafés, bars, and restaurants

PLACE JACQUES-CARTIER AND VIEUX-MONTRÉAL

Vieux-Montréal deserves a two day visit. Start your first day at the Infotouriste building at Place Jacques-Cartier and rue Notre-Dame Est, passing Admiral Lord Horatio Nelson's monument to visit the Musée du Château Ramezay and the Second Empire Hôtel de Ville. Continue on Notre-Dame to visit the Sir George-Étienne Cartier National Historic Site. Turn right on rue Berri and right again on rue Saint-Paul, Vieux-Montréal's curving main street. This will take you past the domed Marché Bonsecours and the Chapelle Notre-Dame, as well as the 18th-century Maison du Calvet, finishing back at Place Jacques-Cartier.

Start the second day again at the Infotouriste but walk away from Place Jacques-Cartier to the Basilique Notre-Dame, Montréal's grandest church, on Place d'Armes with its statue of city founder Paul de Chomedey, Sieur de Maisonneuve. Turn left down rue Saint-François-Xavier past the Old Stock Exchange (now the Centaur, Montréal's leading English-language theatre). Turn right on rue Saint-Paul and then left on rue Saint-Pierre to Place d'Youville and then turn left again to visit the Centre d'Histoire de Montréal and the Musée d'archéologie et d'histoire Pointe-à-Callière. Then stroll along the waterfront of the Vieux-Port back to Place Jacques-Cartier.

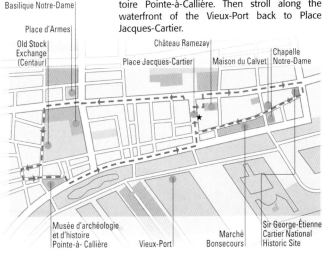

Basilique Notre-Dame
Place d'Armes
Old Stock Exchange (Centaur)
Château Ramezay
Place Jacques-Cartier
Maison du Calvet
Chapelle Notre-Dame
Musée d'archéologie et d'histoire Pointe-à- Callière
Vieux-Port
Marché Bonsecours
Sir George-Étienne Cartier National Historic Site

DOWNTOWN AND THE SQUARE MILE

Start at the Musée d'art contemporain, which houses Canada's finest collection of modern art. Follow signs to rue Sainte-Catherine, stopping at Square Phillips (the statue is King Edward VII) to visit the Anglican Christ Church Cathedral. Continue along rue Sainte-Catherine and turn right on avenue McGill-College, a short, broad avenue with glorious views of Mont-Royal that ends at the gates to the McGill University campus. You can detour right for a block on rue Sherbrooke to visit the McCord Museum at rue Victoria, or turn left and walk through part of the Square Mile, once home to Canada's 19th-century plutocrats. You'll pass many of their fine old houses and churches and the venerable Hôtel Ritz-Carlton before coming to the Musée des beaux-arts at the corner of avenue du Musée. Continue along Sherbrooke to the Grande Séminaire de Montréal at rue du Fort. The two 17th-century stone towers on the grounds, once part of a fort, are among the oldest structures on the island (the interiors are closed to the public). Turn left on rue du Fort and left again on rue Baile to visit the Centre Canadien d'Architecture. Turn left on rue Saint-Marc and right on rue Sainte-Catherine and right again on rue Peel to finish your walk at Square Dorchester and the Roman Catholic Cathédrale Marie-Reine-du-Monde.

SO MUCH TO SEE

The walk takes in four major museums, the McGill University campus, two cathedrals, two churches, and striking modern buildings such as the Maison Alcan. There's shopping at Centre Eaton, Promenades de la Cathédrale, exclusive Holt Renfrew, and the museum boutiques.

INFORMATION

Distance 3km (2mi)
Time 1.5 hours
Start point ★ Musée d'Art Contemporain
➕ F7
🚇 Place des Arts
End point Square-Dorchester
➕ F8
🚇 Peel

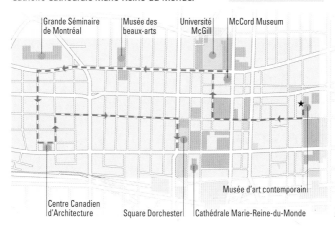

Grande Séminaire de Montréal | Musée des beaux-arts | Université McGill | McCord Museum

Centre Canadien d'Architecture | Square Dorchester | Cathédrale Marie-Reine-du-Monde | Musée d'art contemporain

Montréal by Night

Above left: the nocturnal lure of the Casino de Montréal
Above right: the marina of the Vieux-Port

LONG HISTORY

Montréal has been a popular hot spot with Americans since at least the 1920s and 1930s. During Prohibition, trainloads of fun seekers from New York and Boston would pour into the city every weekend looking for some excitement and a little legal booze. Many of them smuggled a few extra bottles home with them. The city was also popular with African-American jazz musicians, who liked the fact they could pretty much stay and eat wherever they wanted—and date locals without raising much more than an eyebrow.

Montréalers never hibernate, no matter how cold it gets. Saturday-night crowds are almost as large in January as they are in July.

Crowds tend to congregate in two main districts, each with its own ambience and linguistic flavour. In one of these areas—downtown—the scene is mainly on four streets that run between boulevard René-Lévesque and rue Sherbrooke—de la Montagne, Crescent, Bishop, and Mackay. They're lined with fine old greystone residences now converted into pubs, clubs, and bistros, which appeal to a young, hip, and largely English-speaking crowd.

Just as vibrant but more French in ambience is the district around the twin corridors of boulevard Saint-Laurent and rue Saint-Denis. Start around rue Sainte-Catherine and walk away from the river through the Quartier Latin and Plateau Mont-Royal, being sure to explore the cafés and clubs on Prince-Arthur and Rachel. The crowds may be young—the city's population has North America's highest proportion of students—but there's plenty of entertainment for all ages. And the linguistic lines aren't set in stone—you'll find both languages everywhere.

Vieux-Montréal has only a few nightclubs, but it's a wonderful place for an evening stroll. Many of the old classical buildings, including the Hôtel de Ville, Place Royale, and the Château Ramezay—are beautifully illuminated, and a small section of rue Sainte-Hélène is lit by gas lamps.

MONTRÉAL's
top 25 sights

The sights are shown on the maps on the inside front cover and inside back cover, numbered **1**–**25** across the city

Biodôme de Montréal

HIGHLIGHTS

- "Waterbabies"
- Parrots
- Otters
- Lynx
- Penguins

INFORMATION

- G1; locator map off C1
- 4777 avenue Pierre-de-Coubertin
- 514/868-3000; www.ville.montreal.qc.ca/biodome
- Mid-Jun to early Sep: daily 9–7. Early Sep to mid-Jun: daily 9–5
- Café
- Viau
- Very good
- Expensive
- Parc olympique (► 27), Jardin botanique (► 28)
- Gift shop

Sea life enjoyed without having to get wet

The Biôdome has been a success ever since it opened in 1992 in what used to be the Olympic bicycle-racing stadium. This living museum integrates birds, animals, and plants into superb re-creations of their natural habitats.

Habitats   Montréal's Biodôme, the only one of its kind in the world, replicates four of the most beautiful habitats in North, Central, and South America—tropical forest, the St. Lawrence marine ecosystem, Laurentian forest, and the polar world—with their plants, birds, marine creatures, and other animals. You watch otters frolicking in waterfalls, observe marine creatures through glass, and peek at animals and preening birds through the foliage of living forest. But this is more than an indoor zoo. It is actively involved in breeding endangered species in captivity with the hope of releasing the offspring into the wild.

Animals   As you walk into the first habitat, the Amazonian rain forest, heat, humidity, and animal smells hit you like a wall. Exotic birds chirp overhead, while the leafy undergrowth is alive with crocodiles, capybaras (or "waterbaby," one of the world's largest rodents), and golden lion tamarins (orange-furred monkeys that are increasingly scarce in their native Brazil). You'll also see darting parrots, a cave full of bats (behind glass), and other mammals, amphibians, reptiles, and fish. In the Laurentian forest you can watch lynx, otter, beaver, and porcupine. A 2.5-million litre tank in the St. Lawrence marine ecosystem re-creates a miniature sea complete with nesting gannets and a tidal pool filled with anemones and sea urchins. The most popular exhibits—the puffins and penguins—are in the polar area.

Parc Olympique

During the summer 1976 Olympic Games, the perfect performances of Romanian gymnast Nadia Comanecia thrilled the world. But once over, the games left an architectural and financial legacy that still divides the city.

Cost When Mayor Jean Drapeau persuaded Montréalers to host the Olympic Games in 1976 he promised that the likelihood of the event costing them a cent would be about the same as that of a man having a baby. French architect Roger Taillibert set to work believing money was no object. Both were wrong. The stadium and its famous tower cost $1.2 (US) billion, and Québec smokers are still paying off the debt with a special tax on tobacco. Locals now call the stadium the "Big O," partly in reference to its circular shape and because of the huge debt the city ran up to pay for the project. The stadium itself has never been much of a success as a sports venue, abandoned by the local football team, and the Expos, Montréal's major-league baseball team, try also to leave. The place makes its money on trade shows and huge concerts. But it's impressively bright and airy, and worth seeing.

Leaning tower It is not so much the stadium that pulls in visitors, however, it's the park's famous inclined tower (Tour de Montréal), built to support the stadium's retractable roof. Since it opened in 1989, over 4.2 million people have ascended to the observation platform. The 175m (575ft) ascent via an external cable car is stomach churning, but you are rewarded with a mesmerizing view that on a clear day stretches for 80km (50mi). Galleries in the tower's lower levels contain displays about the park's history, and the Tourist Hall at the tower's base has information, tickets, and exhibits.

DID YOU KNOW?

- Completed: 1989
- Years late: 13
- Usage: 250 days a year (world's highest stadium usage)
- Seats: 55,147
- Area: 6ha (14.8 acres)
- Area: space for seven jumbo jets
- World's tallest inclined tower
- Lean: 23–45 degrees
- Weight of cables: 213 tonnes (210 tons)
- Cable car: 270m (886ft) in two minutes

INFORMATION

- ✚ G1; locator map off C1
- ✉ 4141 avenue Pierre-de-Coubertin
- ☎ 514/252-8687; www.rio.gouv.qc.ca
- 🕐 12 Jun–early Sep: Mon 12–9; Tue–Sun 10–9. Mid-Sep to 9 Jan, 12 Feb–early Jun, and hols: Mon 12–5; Tue–Sun 11–5. Guided tours in French daily 11 and 2; in English 12.40 and 3.40
- 🍴 Cafés
- Ⓥ Viau
- 🚌 185
- ♿ Very good
- ↔ Biodôme de Montréal (►26), Jardin botanique (►28)
- ❓ Souvenir shop

27

Jardin Botanique de Montréal

DID YOU KNOW?

- Area: 75ha (185 acres)
- Flora: 26,000 species
- Specimens: 36,000
- Bonsai: largest collection in North America
- Insects in L'Insectarium: 149,000; on display 20,000
- Muscles in a house fly: 5,000

INFORMATION

- ✚ G1; locator map off C1
- ✉ Jardin botanique, 4101 rue Sherbrooke Est; Insectarium, 4581 rue Sherbrooke Est
- ☎ Jardin botanique 514/872-1400; www.ville.montreal.qc.ca/jardin. L'Insectarium 514/868-3056; www.ville.montreal.qc.ca/insectarium
- 🕐 Late Jun–early Sep: daily 9–7. Mid-Sep to mid-Jun: daily 9–5
- 🍴 Café
- 🚇 Viau, Pie IX
- ♿ Very good
- 💵 Moderate (combined ticket available with Biodôme)
- ↔ Biodôme de Montréal (► 26), Parc olympique (► 27)
- 🚌 Free shuttle bus from Le Biodôme and Viau Métro.

The Montréal-Shanghai Dream Lake Garden

Montréal has the world's second-largest botanical gardens—no small feat given the cruel climate. The preserve is a blend of exotic horticulture with the beauty and tranquility of a formal garden.

Gardens Montréal's lovely botanical gardens are the second largest in the world after Kew Gardens in London. Opened in 1931, they now comprise some 30 different outdoor gardens and 10 vast exhibition greenhouses. Each garden represents a different climate, country or style, ranging from a collection of poisonous plants to gardens devoted to orchids or medicinal herbs. Nearby lies the Insectarium, in a suitably bug-shaped building. Its galleries are filled with all manner of displays and countless insects living and dead (and exotic butterflies in summer). Don't miss the gargantuan South American cockroaches. And in February visitors can try some truly high-protein morsels as local cooks whip up chocolate-covered ants, honey-dipped bees, and the ever popular bug-centred lollipops.

Shanghai surprise The gardens' highlight is the 1991 2ha (6-acre) Montréal-Shanghai Dream Lake Garden, a perfect replica of one from the Ming dynasty (1368–1644), and designed to celebrate the friendship between the two cities. Lakes, rocks, and plants strive for a harmonious blend of *yin* and *yang*: small and large, soft and hard, light and dark, flowing and immovable. Look for the seven elegant pavilions, central reflecting pool, large rockery, and collection of miniature trees known as "penjings" (on display in summer only). Also exquisite is the Japanese Garden and Pavilion, home to a minimalist mineral Zen garden, as well as a summer collection of Japanese bonsai trees.

Parc du Mont-Royal

Mont-Royal is only 233m (764ft) above sea level but Montréalers call it, without irony, "the Mountain," an appropriately grand appellation given the hold this steep, green oasis has on their affection.

History Mont-Royal is one of seven such peaks on the St. Lawrence plain, all composed of intrusive rock hard enough to have survived the glacial scraping of the last Ice Age. Explorer Jacques Cartier named the hill—probably in honour of his royal patron, Francis I of France—on his first voyage up the St. Lawrence in 1535. The area became a park in 1877, following the local council's fear (after a particularly severe winter) that the forested slopes were being denuded by Montréalers' quest for firewood. The land was bought for $1 million, and landscaped by designer Frederick Law Olmsted, also responsible for New York's Central Park and San Francisco's Golden Gate Park.

Attractions The park is too large to see in a day, so pick a corner to explore. A bicycle gives more opportunities for seeing further afield. Most people on foot enter at the Monument Sir-George-Étienne-Cartier, a popular summer venue for street musicians, vendors, and people-watchers. Olmsted Road leads to the famous Montréal Cross (1924) on the summit. Beaver Lake, created in the 1930s, is another focal point, as is Le Chalet, which has fantastic views and an interpretative centre. Calixa Lavallée, composer of Canada's national anthem, is buried in the Roman Catholic Cimetière Notre-Dame-des-Neiges, one of two huge cemeteries on the park's northern perimeter, and Ann Leonowens, immortalized in *The King and I*, is in the Protestant Mont-Royal Cemetery.

HIGHLIGHTS

- Montréal Cross
- Le Chalet viewpoint
- Beaver Lake
- Notre Dame des Neiges Cemetery
- Mont-Royal Cemetery

INFORMATION

- ✚ B8–E6; locator map A1
- ✉ Monument Sir-George-Étienne-Cartier and other entrances
- ☎ 514/843-8240; www.lemontroyal.com
- 🕐 Daily 6AM–midnight
- 🍴 The Chalet
- 🚇 Mont-Royal
- 🚌 11, 66, 80, 107, 129, 144, 165
- ♿ Some steep paths
- 🎫 Free
- ↔ Oratoire Saint-Joseph (► 30), Musée des beaux-arts (► 33), McCord Museum (► 32)

DID YOU KNOW?

- Area: 203ha (500 acres)
- Paths: 56km (35mi)
- Ski paths: 19km (12mi)
- Bodies in cemeteries: 1 million plus
- Height of Montréal Cross: 30m (98ft)
- Distance cross is visible when lit: over 88km (55mi)

Oratoire Saint-Joseph

The dome of the Oratoire Saint-Joseph, one of the world's largest, is a distinctive landmark on the Montréal skyline, and the church beneath it is the most important Roman Catholic shrine dedicated to Christ's earthly father.

The oratory's vast dome

DID YOU KNOW?

- Height: 260m (853ft)
- Seating capacity: 3,200 (standing 10,000)
- Christmas cribs: over 30
- From: 103 countries

INFORMATION

- B8; locator map off A3
- 3800 chemin Queen Mary near Côtes-des-Neiges
- 514/733-8211; www.saint-joseph.org
- Daily 9–5
- Café
- Côte-des-Neiges
- 51, 144, 165, 166, 535 (peak hours)
- Very good
- Oratory free. Museum guided tours inexpensive
- Parc du Mont-Royal (► 29)

Miracle cures The story of the Oratoire Saint-Joseph begins with Brother André Bessette, a diminutive, barely literate man born in 1837 to a poor rural family. He joined a religious order—the Congrégation du Saint-Croix—and worked as a porter in the order's classical college at the foot of Mont-Royal. He built a small shrine to his favourite saint on the mountain slopes and cared for sick pilgrims. He developed an extraordinary reputation as a healer, and donations began to pour into the order from grateful pilgrims who wanted to help André fulfill his dream of building a grand monument to St. Joseph. Construction began in 1924 and Brother André lived long enough to see the completion of the crypt, but the main church with its dome was not finished until 1937, long after his death.

Interior André was beatified in 1982 and buried in the oratory, which also includes part of his original chapel, a small museum about his life, the room in which he died (removed wholesale from a local hospice), and his preserved heart (occasionally said to quiver miraculously). The 56-bell carillon was originally cast for the Eiffel Tower but never installed; the bells were loaned to the oratory in 1955 and later bought. There are free carillon and organ recitals year round. Be sure to climb to the observatory, one of Montréal's highest points, for a superb view, and to study the fine Carrera marble sculptures marking the Stations of the Cross outside in Mont-Royal.

McGill University

If you stand on the stone steps of McGill's glass-and-concrete Leacock Building when the snow is falling, and look out across the whitened campus at the glittering city towers, you could fall in love with winter.

Urban country   The university opened in 1821, far from the city limits on Mont-Royal's lower slopes, on a patch of pasture donated for the purpose by fur trader and land speculator James McGill. Since then, Montréal has spread inexorably northwards and now surrounds the 32ha (80-acre) campus. McGill offers not so much a respite from the city as a privileged place from which to view it and feel its vibrant rhythms.

Architecture   The Greek Revival Roddick Gates guard the main entrance to the university on rue Sherbrooke Ouest, and behind them a long tree-lined avenue leads to the 1839 neoclassical domed Arts Building, the oldest of the 70 or so buildings on campus. Inside is Moyse Hall, a lovely theatre dating from 1926. Along the avenue's east side are two fine neoclassical buildings designed by Sir Andrew Taylor in the 1890s, who also designed the Library with its elaborately carved columns and gargoyles. Percy Nobbs's 1908 Macdonald Engineering Building is a remarkable example of the English Baroque Revival style. But the most beautiful structure on campus is the temple-like Redpath Museum of Natural History, refurbished in 2001 and one of Canada's oldest museums; it houses a huge and wonderfully whimsical collection that includes dinosaur bones, old coins, African art, and a shrunken head. On the lawn outside is a fine stone fountain, and under the trees a bronze James McGill hurries across campus holding his tricorn hat against the wind.

HIGHLIGHTS

- Roddick Gates
- Green space
- Redpath Museum
- Views
- Arts Building

INFORMATION

- ✚ E7; locator map A2
- ✉ 805 rue Sherbrooke Ouest
- ☎ Redpath Museum 514/398-4086; www.mcgill.ca
- 🕐 Sep–May: Mon–Fri 9–5; Sun 1–5. Jun–Aug: Mon–Thu 9–5; Sun 1–5
- Ⓜ McGill
- ♿ Fair
- 🎫 Free
- ↔ Parc du Mont-Royal (► 29), McCord Museum (► 32), Musée des beaux-arts (► 33), Christ Church Cathedral (► 35)

Outside the Macdonald Engineering Building

McCord Museum

One of Canada's best museums, the McCord Museum of Canadian History possesses a huge breadth of artefacts, including Native Canadian culture, an important photographic collection, which provide a fascinating insight into Montréal's past.

INFORMATION

- E7; locator map B2
- 690 rue Sherbrooke Ouest at rue Victoria
- 514/398-7100; www.musee-mccord.qc.ca
- Mon and hols 10–6; Tue–Fri 10–6; Sat, Sun 10–5
- The McCord Café
- McGill
- 24, 125
- Good
- Moderate (free Sat 10–12)
- McGill University (➤ 31), Musée des beaux-arts (➤ 33), Christ Church Cathedral (➤ 35), Musée d'art contemporain (➤ 38)
- Guided tours, reading room

A Native Canadian totem pole

Museum Montréal lawyer David Ross McCord (1844–1930), the scion of a prosperous Scots-Irish family, was a collector with an insatiable appetite for anything with Canadian history. In the 1920s he gave his huge collection of books, furniture, clothing, guns, paintings, documents, toys, and photographs to McGill University, where it was housed in the McGill Union Building (1906). A $20-million renovation in 1992 doubled the museum's size, but still there is space to display only a fragment of its 90,000-piece collection.

Photographs The museum is strongest on the culture and history of Native Canadians, or First Peoples, and devotes several galleries to native furs, carvings, and embroidered beadwork. The collections also include some 10,000 costumes, many dating from the 18th century and earlier. Also remarkable is the Notman Archives, a collection of prints and glass prints produced by photographic pioneer William Notman, who captured Victorian life in Montréal. The photographs include formal balls, soldiers marching, and members of the exclusive Montréal Athletic Association in snowshoes. Each of the hundreds of people shown in these pictures was photographed individually in the studio and then painstakingly mounted on the appropriate background.

Musée des Beaux-Arts

Canada's oldest art museum (founded in 1860) consists of the Museum of Fine Arts and its magnificent new Desmarais Pavilion, and has the best collection of Canadian paintings in the country, as well as Native Canadian artefacts, and many fine Old Masters.

Museum Radical alterations have made this venerable institution one of North America's finest galleries. Completed in 1912 and enlarged in 1976, the main building is an unmistakable feature of rue Sherbrooke, with its stolid Vermont marble front and four enormous Ionic columns. Across the street stands the Desmarais Pavilion (1991), a stunning modern building designed by well-known Montréal architect Moshe Safdie. Wonderful views across the city open up from its upper levels, and underground galleries connect it with the original building.

Collection Canadian paintings range from works imported by the earliest French settlers through to those by artists from the Toronto-based Group of Seven. Look for the fine landscapes, and for paintings by the so-called Automatistes, who dominated Montréal's art world during the 1940s. Many Native Canadian artefacts are on display, along with period furnishings, drawings, engravings, silverware, and art from ancient China, Japan, Egypt, Greece, and South America. Among the old masters originally bought by wealthy Montréal fur traders are paintings by Rembrandt, El Greco, and Memlinc; works by Picasso, Henry Moore, and Impressionists represent more recent eras. The museum has absorbed the defunct Musée des arts décoratifs and now displays its superb collection of ceramics, fabrics, and furniture.

HIGHLIGHTS

- *Portrait of a Young Woman*, Rembrandt
- *Portrait of a Man*, El Greco
- *Torso*, Henry Moore
- *October*, James Tissot

James Tissot's October

INFORMATION

- ✚ E8; locator map off A3
- ✉ 1379 rue Sherbrooke Ouest
- ☎ 514/285-1600; www.mmfa.qc.ca
- ◷ Tue, Thu–Sun 11–6; Wed 11–9
- 🍴 Café du Musée, Le Mitoyen restaurant
- Ⓖ Guy-Concordia
- 🚌 24
- ♿ Good
- 📖 Free permanent exhibition. Special shows expensive

33

Canadian Centre for Architecture

INFORMATION

- E8; locator map off A4
- 1920 rue Baile between rues Saint-Marc and du Fort
- 514/939-7026; www.cca.qc.ca
- Jun–Sep: Tue, Wed, Fri–Sun 11–6; Thu 11–8. Oct–May: Wed, Fri 11–6; Thu 11–8; Sat, Sun 11–5
- Guy-Concordia, Atwater
- 15, 150, 535
- Excellent
- Centre moderate (free Thu 6–8). Sculpture Gardens free
- Musée des beaux-arts (➤ 33)
- Guided tours of building and gardens Sun 2.30 (French), 3.30 (English)

DID YOU KNOW?

- Books: 195,000
- Photographs: 60,000
- Prints and drawings: 70,000
- Periodicals: 700

There's something fitting about the layout of what is arguably the world's premier architectural museum. Its U-plan fortress embraces an impressive 19th-century mansion built for one of Montréal's great plutocrats.

Temple of architecture The grey limestone facade is not terribly welcoming. Long and low, it is virtually windowless, and the front door, at the building's western end, appears an afterthought. But that door leads into six beautifully lit halls given over to changing exhibits ranging from the academic to the whimsical—displays on modernist theory and American lawn culture are equally at home. Incorporated into the complex is the 1877 Shaughnessy Mansion, with its wonderful art nouveau conservatory, built for Canadian Pacific Railway chairman Sir Thomas Shaughnessy. Across the street, in a little island of green between two busy main thoroughfares, is a garden designed by Melvin Charney, where fanciful fragments—a set of Doric columns here, a Victorian doorway there—tell the story of architecture.

History The woman behind all this is architect Phyllis Lambert. A fierce defender of Montréal's architectural heritage, she founded the centre in 1979 and presided, with architect Peter Rose, over the building of its present home (1985–89). She also contributed her own impressive collection to the centre—65,000 prints and drawings (some by Michelangelo and Leonardo da Vinci), 50,000 architectural photographs, and 180,000 books and publications dating from 15th-century manuscripts to the present. The collection forms the backbone of the centre's archives, which are open by appointment.

Christ Church Cathedral

The seat of Montréal's Anglican bishop is a graceful ship of serenity floating (almost literally) on a sea of commerce. There are department stores on either side of it, a skyscraper behind, and a shopping mall right underneath.

Top: the world beneath the cathedral
Above: the cathedral, dwarfed by skyscrapers

Copy This beautifully simple church is the city's Anglican cathedral, built between 1857 and 1859 at the instigation of Francis Fulford, Montréal's first Anglican bishop. Its neo-Gothic style is reminiscent of a 14th-century English church, but its plan is actually a straight copy of the Anglican cathedral in Fredericton, N. B., which was designed by the same architect Frank Wills. It was originally faced with stone imported from Caen in Normandy, but was replaced with Indiana limestone. The steeple had problems too. It was too heavy for the soft, unstable ground and was replaced in 1927 with one made of aluminium plates, craftily doctored to match the stone of the rest of the church. Among the notable artefacts inside the church is a cross made from nails rescued from the bombed Coventry Cathedral in England.

Money matters Over time soaring towers have dwarfed the cathedral, while high maintenance costs and dwindling congregations led to a budgetary shortfall. The Anglican authorities found an imaginative solution in 1985 when they leased the land around and beneath the cathedral to developers. Ground under the building was removed, leaving the church supported by metal girders and balanced precariously above a yawning chasm; the church now sits atop Les Promenades de la Cathédrale, a busy mall. Shoppers, office workers, and store clerks of all faiths retreat to the cathedral at midday for free concerts and organ recitals.

INFORMATION

* ✚ F7; locator map B3
* ✉ 635 rue Sainte-Catherine Ouest and avenue Union
* ☎ Recorded information 514/288-6421. Cathedral staff 514/843-6577; www.montreal.anglican.org/cathedral
* 🕐 Daily 8–6
* Ⓜ McGill
* ♿ Very good; ramps from street
* 🎟 Free
* ↔ McGill University (► 31), McCord Museum (► 32), Musée des beaux-arts (► 33), Cathédrale Marie-Reine-du-Monde (► 37), Musée d'art contemporain (► 38)
* ❓ Midday and evening choral and organ concerts

35

Underground City

INFORMATION

- E7–F8; locator map C3
- Access at Métro stations in the city centre
- Sun–Fri 5.30AM–12.30AM; Sat 5.30AM–1AM
- Peel, McGill, Bonaventure, Place-des-Arts, Square-Victoria

It's possible to arrive in Montréal by train in winter and spend a pleasant week without once stepping outside. You could shop, dine, see an opera, go to church, or even watch a hockey game without putting on your coat.

Beginnings   Montréal's vast underground city began modestly enough in the early 1960s, when a mall full of shops and boutiques opened underneath the main plaza of Place Ville-Marie, the city's first modern skyscraper. Both it and the neighbouring Queen Elizabeth Hotel were built over the Canadian National Railway's tracks so it seemed natural enough to link both of them with Central Station, and to Place Bonaventure to the south. The idea caught on, not surprisingly in a city with bitter winters and humid summers, and really took off when the Métro opened in 1966.

Growth   The underground now has more than 29km (18mi) of wide, well-lit tunnels, mostly clustered around 10 of the 64km (40mi) Métro system's 65 stations. At last count, the system encompassed seven major hotels, two universities, both train stations, more than 1,600 boutiques, two department stores, more than 200 restaurants, at least 30 cinemas, the Olympic Stadium, and the Molson Centre. The only universities are French: The Université de Montréal and the Université du Québec à Montréal (UQAM). Oddly in a city that was once so Roman Catholic, the only church with its own link to the system is the Protestant Christ Church Cathedral. Remember that only the links are underground: Most of the shops and malls are above ground. In fact, the soaring glass lobby of Place des Arts is as much a part of the system as the deepest Métro station.

Top: inside the Desjardins complex
Above: Métro entrance

Cathédrale Marie-Reine-du-Monde

Mary Queen of the World Cathedral brings the Italian Renaissance into the heart of Montréal. Dwarfed now by skyscrapers, the cathedral was a daring monument to 19th-century Roman Catholic triumphalism.

Looking up into the dome of the cathedral

Imitation Bishop Ignace Bourget, who began the cathedral three years after Canadian confederation into the Dominion, intended to underline papal supremacy and show that Catholicism still dominated what was then the largest city in the Dominion. So he set the cathedral at the heart of the city's Anglo-Protestant district, and designed it as a one-quarter-size replica of St. Peter's in Rome. Begun in 1870, the building was completed in 1894. The figures outside, often mistaken for the Apostles, represent the patron saints of parishes in the Archdiocese of Montréal.

Interior In contrast to the lovely intimacy of Notre-Dame in Vieux-Montréal, the interior is sombre, although the interiors of both churches are the work of architect Victor Bourgeau. The gloom was intended to intensify the effect of candles and accentuate the rose windows. The opulent high altar features a copy of the vast baldacchino, or altar canopy, by Bernini in St. Peter's, while the first little chapel in the left aisle has a red-flocked sanctuary filled with medals and saintly relics. Bishop Bourget is interred in a second chapel on the same side of the church, his recumbent figure surrounded by the tombs of his successors. One last sign of Montréal's loyalty to the Holy See is mounted on a pillar facing the bishop's tomb—a memorial to the men from the diocese who served in the Papal Zouaves in the fight against Italian nationalists.

HIGHLIGHTS

- Stained glass
- High altar
- Bourget Chapel

INFORMATION

- ✚ F8; locator map C3
- ✉ Boulevard René-Lévesque Ouest and rue Mansfield
- ☎ 514/866-1661
- 🕐 Daily 7–7
- Ⓜ Bonaventure
- 🚌 38, 107, 150, 410, 420, 535
- ♿ Very good: steep ramp
- 💷 Free
- ↔ Christ Church Cathedral (▶ 35), St. Patrick's Basilica (▶ 39)

37

Musée d'Art Contemporain

HIGHLIGHTS

- Architecture
- *Lips*, Geneviève Cadieux
- Steel atrium
- Sculpture garden
- Paul-Émile Borduas, *L'Île fortifiée*

INFORMATION

- F7; locator map C2
- 185 rue Sainte-Catherine Ouest at rue Jeanne-Mance
- 514/847-6226
- Tue, Thu–Sun 11–6; Wed 11–9
- La Rotonde restaurant (lunch, dinner)
- Place-des-Arts
- 15, 55, 86, 129
- Very good
- Moderate; free Wed from 6PM for collection; reduced rate for exhibitions
- McCord Museum (➤ 32), Christ Church Cathedral (➤ 35), St. Patrick's Basilica (➤ 39)
- Guided tours, weekend schedule, and child activities

A pair of billboard-size lips—illuminated at night—marks Canada's only major museum of contemporary art. The building is just as impressive, from its offbeat doors to the distinctive angular galleries and central atrium.

Building   Founded in 1964 by the Québec government, the museum occupied three different buildings before moving into its present home, a superb plain-faced modern building only a stone's throw from Place des Arts (➤ 83), in 1992. It originally focused on the work of indigenous Québécois artists, but the museum has increasingly widened its scope and now mounts temporary exhibitions of work by artists from all around the world. It has hosted well over 600 exhibitions, and attracted some 1.6 million visitors.

Paintings   Works of art in the gallery date from around 1939 up to the present, with at least 60 percent of the more than 5,000 works of art in the museum's collection Québécois artists. Among those represented are David Moore, Alfred Pellan, Jean-Paul Riopelle, with 75 paintings by Montréal artist Paul-Émile Borduas on view. Canadian artists include Jack Bush, Michael Snow, and Barbara Steinman. Works by Picasso, Lichtenstein, and Warhol are also on display. There is a growing video art collection, started in 1979. Much of the permanent collection is often moved out to make way for temporary exhibitions, such as retrospectives of the work of Guido Molinari, one of Canada's leading abstract artists, and Henry Saxe, one of the country's foremost sculptors, and exhibitions of recent acquisitions. Remember to look round the impressive sculpture garden, which includes work by Pierre Granche.

St. Patrick's Basilica

Visitors arrive by the busload to see the Basilique Notre-Dame-de-Montréal. Just a few blocks north, the pious and the knowledgeable have the delicate gold and green beauty of St. Patrick's Basilica to themselves.

History Bishop Ignace Bourget gave only grudging approval when the Irish Catholics of his diocese asked for a church of their own in 1843. The mass, he reasoned, was in Latin, and most of the Irish spoke Gaelic at home, not English. Surely they could go to church with their French-speaking brethren. But the Irish persisted and with help from the Sulpician priests erected one of Canada's most graceful neo-Gothic churches.

Features On sunny afternoons, light floods through the stained-glass figures of the four evangelists, and fills the soaring nave with a honey-coloured glow. The vault over the sanctuary gleams with green and gold mosaics and the air smells of a mixture of beeswax polish and incense. The pulpit is decorated with panels of the 12 apostles, a huge sanctuary lamp is graced with a half-dozen 2m (6ft) angels, and poet Emile Nelligan was baptized in the ornate font. But what sets the church apart is the overwhelming presence of the communion of saints. Dozens of statues of bishops, martyrs, missionaries, princesses, and peasants jostle for space on the main altar and crowd the niches of the side altars. Another 150 holy men and women are honoured in painted panels that line the walls of the nave. And at least one of the fathers of the confederation of Canada is remembered, as well. Parishioner Thomas Darcy McGee was buried from St. Patrick's after his assassination in 1868. His pew (No. 240) is towards the back, marked with a Canadian flag.

Top **25**

14

HIGHLIGHTS

- Pulpit
- Sanctuary lamp
- Darcy McGee's pew

INFORMATION

- ✚ F7; locator map C3
- ✉ 460 boulevard René-Lévesque Ouest
- ☎ 514/866-7379; www.sympatico.ca/stpatrickmtl
- ◉ Daily 9–6
- Ⓜ McGill
- ♿ Fair
- 🎫 Free
- ↔ Christ Church Cathedral (► 35), Cathédrale Marie-Reine-du-Monde (► 37), Basilique Notre-Dame (► 40)

Top and above: the saintly embellishments of the main altar

Basilique Notre-Dame

HIGHLIGHTS

- Pulpit
- Wood carving
- Stained glass
- High altar

INFORMATION

- G7; locator map E3
- 110 rue Notre-Dame Ouest
- Basilica 514/842-2925
- Late Jun–early Sep: daily 7AM–8PM. Late Sep–early Jun: daily 7–6
- Place-d'Armes
- 38, 55, 129
- Very good
- Moderate
- St. Patrick's Basilica (➤ 39), Centre d'histoire de Montréal (➤ 41), Musée d'archéologie (➤ 42), Vieux-Port de Montréal (➤ 47)
- Guided tours mid-May to late Jun and early Sep to mid-Oct: daily 9–4.30 every half-hour

DID YOU KNOW?

- Seats: 3,500
- Standing: 2,000
- Bell-ringers once required: 12
- Organ pipes: 7,000

No other site in Montréal sums up the city's religious heritage as beautifully as the Basilica of Notre Dame, where the seductive interior—Romanesque with touches of rococo—lifts you into a world of almost perfect calm.

History Founded in 1627, Notre-Dame is on the flanks of Place d'Armes, long the historic focus of the old city. The original church was replaced by the present neo-Gothic basilica between 1824 and 1829, and it was the largest religious building in North America when it was inaugurated. Today there is a skyscraper on the square's western side, but the church's twin towers—nicknamed Temperance and Perseverance—still command the skyline. The western tower, built in 1843, contains the famous "Gros Bourdon," a 12.2-tonne (12-ton) bell, whose peal can be heard up to 25km (15mi) away.

Highly decorated Inside, thousands of tiny 24-carat gold stars stud the dusky blue, vaulted ceiling, and 14 stained-glass windows, brought from Limoges in 1929, tell the story of Ville-Marie's early development. But most of the interior is a tribute to the woodworking skills of Québec artists and artisans. All the figures in the life-size tableaux behind the main altar are carved in wood as is the spectacular pulpit with its curving staircase on the east side of the nave. A fire in 1978 destroyed much of the large chapel behind the main altar. The Sulpician priests who run the church saved what they could of the original ornate woodwork and erected an enormous, modern bronze sculpture behind the altar. The chapel is still the most popular for weddings in Montréal; in 1994 pop diva Céline Dion married her manager in a ceremony that rivalled the pomp of a royal wedding.

Centre d'Histoire de Montréal

Although this history museum seems a little dated at first glance, it tells Montréal's story in a charming way, allowing you to step in and share snippets of Montréalers' day-to-day lives from 1642 to the present.

History Of the monuments and historic sites that line Place d'Youville, one of Montréal's earliest market squares, the most attractive is the beautifully restored red stone Caserne Centrale de Pompiers, or old Central Fire Station (1903). Today this building houses the Centre d'histoire de Montréal, an 11-room interpretative centre which uses dioramas, videos, and other media to trace the city's development from Iroquois settlement to present-day metropolis. Look for the mock-ups of the streetcar, the 19th-century factory, and the gaudy 1940s living room. Temporary exhibitions on offbeat aspects of the city's history are often held upstairs.

Also on the square On the south side of Place d'Youville stand the Youville Stables (Écuries d'Youville), greystone buildings constructed in 1828 as warehouses for grain merchants and soap manufacturers (the stables were next door). In 1967 the complex was converted into an attractive mixture of offices, shops, and artisans' studios. Just off the square a plaque commemorates the Hôpital Général des Sœurs-Grises (Gray Nuns' General Hospital), founded in 1694 as the city's second hospital and taken over in 1747 by Marguerite d'Youville, the wealthy widow who founded the Sœurs Grises. The order treated Montréal's sick, poor, and elderly and established one of North America's first foundling hospitals. Part of the original foundation survives off rue Saint-Pierre.

HIGHLIGHTS

- Fire Station building
- Tram car
- Youville Stables

INFORMATION

- G7; locator map E3
- 335 place d'Youville
- 514/872-3207; www.ville.montreal.qc.ca/chm
- May–early Sep: daily 10–5. Early Sep–early Dec, mid-Jan to Apr: Tue–Sun 10–5
- Square-Victoria
- 38, 55, 61
- Moderate
- Basilique Notre-Dame (► 40), Pointe-à-Callière (► 42), Vieux-Port de Montréal (► 47)
- Guided tours need to be arranged in advance

Below: tracing the city's development in the Centre d'histoire

Pointe-à-Callière

The Musée d'archéologie et d'histoire de Montréal

Of all the innovations in the Vieux-Port, the superb Musée d'archéologie et d'histoire de Montréal at Pointe-à-Callière is the most impressive. It is the best of the developments that have given a little heart to old Montréal.

Archeology and history   Visit this magnificent modern museum on your first morning in Montréal: Not only does it provide a fascinating introduction to the city's history, but it is also built at Pointe-à-Callière, the city's birthplace. Montréal's first 53 settlers landed on this spot from France on 17 May 1642. The museum uses audiovisual displays to tell the story of Montréal's development as a trading and meeting place.

Underground   The main building of this $27-million museum is the stark, ship-like Édifice de l'Eperon, built on the foundations of the Royal Insurance building. It houses offices, temporary exhibits, a café with wonderful river views, and a theatre with a 16-minute multimedia show on Montréal's history. But its real treasures are underground. The museum gives access to the excavations underneath, where archaeologist have burrowed into the silt and rock to expose the layers of the past. They've uncovered the remnants of a 19th-century sewer system, 18th-century tavern foundations, and a cemetery dating to 1643. As you explore, you have virtual encounters with some of the city's more colourful citizens. Tunnels connect the excavations to the neoclassical Old Customs House, where there are still more exhibits and an extensive gift shop. The museum also incorporates the Company 4 Pumphouse, the city's first electrical water-pumping system. It is now an exhibit on industrial development.

Château Ramezay

French governors, British conquerors, and American generals have all stayed in this relic of the French regime. With its squat round towers and its rough stone finish, Château Ramezay is like a bit of Normandy in North America.

History One of North America's most venerable buildings, this Norman-style country house was commissioned in 1705 by Claude de Ramezay, 11th governor of Montréal, and was the work of master mason Pierre Couturier, one of the leading architects of his day (the distinctive round tower was a 19th-century addition). In 1745 de Ramezay's heir sold the property to governors of the Compagnie des Indes (West Indies Company), a fur-trading company that had the monopoly on beaver pelts sold in French North America until the coming of the British. Under the French the house became the city's most fashionable meeting place.

Museum After 1763 the building became home to the Governors General of British North America (1764–1849), and during the brief American invasion of 1775 served as a military headquarters for American commanders Benedict Arnold and Richard Montgomery. Benjamin Franklin was here later the same year, engaged in a doomed attempt to persuade Montréalers to join the US. In 1895 the house was bought and turned into a museum, its interior fitted and furnished as it might have been in the 18th century with paintings, costumes, and furniture. The kitchen, one of the most appealing parts of the house, is filled with period utensils, and the intricate carving of the wood-panelled Grande Salle is a tactile reminder of the opulence of 18th-century Montréal.

HIGHLIGHTS

- Grande Salle
- Portraits
- Kitchen

INFORMATION

- ✚ G6; locator map F2
- ✉ 280 rue Notre-Dame Est at rue Saint-Claude
- ☎ 514/861-3708; www.chateauramezay.ca
- 🕐 Jun–Sep: daily 10–6. Oct–May: Tue–Sun 10–4.30
- 🚇 Champ-de-Mars
- 🚌 38
- ♿ Poor: Ramp can be arranged, so visitors using wheelchairs should phone in advance
- 💰 Moderate
- ↔ Lieu historique national Sir-G.-É. Cartier (➤ 44), Chapelle Notre-Dame-de-Bonsecours (➤ 45), Vieux-Port (➤ 47)
- ❓ Chamber concerts: last Sun of month at 1.30, 2.30, 3.30. Gift shop

Lieu Historique Sir G.-É. Cartier

HIGHLIGHTS

- Commentaries
- Sound effects
- Life-size models
- Canopied bed

INFORMATION

- ✚ G6; locator map F1
- ✉ 458 rue Notre-Dame Est at the corner of rue Berri
- ☎ 514/283-2282
- 🕐 Mid-Jun to Aug: daily 10–6. Early Apr to mid-Jun, Sep–Dec: Wed–Sun 10–12, 1–5
- 🚇 Champ-de-Mars
- 🚌 38
- ♿ Very good, though visitors using wheelchairs should call one day in advance
- 🎙 Inexpensive
- ↔ Château Ramezay (➤ 43), Chapelle Notre-Dame-de-Bonsecours (➤ 45), Marché Bonsecours (➤ 46), Vieux-Port (➤ 47)
- ❓ Guided tours

With great charm, numerous original furnishings and artefacts beautifully re-create the ambience of domestic life in mid 19th-century Montréal in the former home of Sir George-Étienne Cartier (1814–1873).

Cartier Sir George-Étienne Cartier, one of the founding fathers of Canadian confederation, played a large part in persuading French Canada to join the fledgling nation in 1867. In his youth Cartier had thrown his support behind the abortive 1837 rebellion against British rule, but later he became convinced that the new Canadian federation would give French Canadians the means they needed to safeguard their religion, language, and culture.

Museum The museum consists of two connected houses, both of which were home to the Cartier family between 1848 and 1872. The western half concerns itself with Cartier's political and industrial preoccupations. He successfully promoted the construction of the Grand Trunk Railway; he worked on the abolition of Québec's seigneurial system (a hangover from the French regime) and the rewriting of its civil code; and he was Canada's first minister of defence. In one exhibit, you can sit in at a negotiating session with Cartier and the other Fathers of Confederation. The house on the east side of the museum uses ornate period furnishings to re-create the bourgeois life of the Cartier family in 19th-century Montréal. You can also listen in on the servants gossiping about their masters.

Chapelle Notre-Dame-de-Bonsecours

This tiny building is a monument to Marguerite Bourgeoys, a pious woman dedicated to bringing Christian civilization to New France. She founded a religious order, set up schools, and built this church.

Church St. Marguerite Bourgeoys picked the site for the chapel in 1657, just outside Ville-Marie's stockade, and persuaded Montréal's founder, Paul de Chomedey, Sieur de Maisonneuve, to help with the project. Legend has it that he helped cut the timber. The original building was destroyed by fire, and the present stone edifice dates to 1771. The 1998 renovation revealed some beautiful 18th-century murals that had been covered by more recent pictures.

Sailors The chapel has always had a special place in the hearts of mariners. Situated on the waterfront, it was built to house a small 17th-century statue of Notre Dame de Bonsecours (Our Lady of Good Hope), credited with the rescue of those in peril at sea. A larger-than-life statue of the Virgin graces the steeple of the present building, facing the river with arms outstretched in welcome. Mariners who survived the perils of ocean crossings in the 18th and 19th centuries often came to the church to thank the Virgin for her help, and to leave votive lamps in the shape of small model ships. Many of them still hang from the ceiling and the chapel is usually referred to simply as the Église des Matelots, the Sailors' Church. Visitors can climb the steeple to the "Aerial," a tiny chapel where mariners came to pray for safe passage. There is a museum, also renovated in 1998, where you can learn more about the life of St. Marguerite Bourgeoys.

HIGHLIGHTS

- Gold Madonna
- Murals
- Votive boats
- Mosaic inlays
- Madonna de Bonsecours
- "Aerial"
- Views

INFORMATION

- G6; locator map F2
- 400 rue Saint-Paul Est
- 514/845-9991; www.marguerite-bourgeoys.com
- May–Oct: Tue–Sun 10–5. Nov–Apr: Tue–Sun 11–3.30
- Champ-de-Mars
- 38
- Poor: four steps to church; no access to tower or museum
- Church free. Museum inexpensive
- Château Ramezay (► 43), Lieu historique national Sir-G.-É. Cartier (► 44), Marché Bonsecours (► 46)
- Small gift shop

Marché Bonsecours

HIGHLIGHTS

- Silver dome
- Facade
- Portico

INFORMATION

- G6; locator map F2
- 350 rue Saint-Paul Est at rue Bonsecours
- 514/872-7730; www.marchebonsecours. qc.ca
- Sat–Wed 10–6; Thu, Fri 10–9. Exhibition halls 10–6
- Champ-de-Mars
- 38
- Very good
- Free
- Château Ramezay (► 43), Lieu historique national Sir-G.-É. Cartier (► 44), Chapelle Notre-Dame-de-Bonsecours (► 45), Vieux-Port (► 47)

The silvery dome of the Marché Bonsecours has been a landmark on the Montréal waterfront for well over a century. It serves as a reminder of the city's importance as a busy port during the 19th century.

History The site of the Marché Bonsecours was important in 18th-century New France. Colonial authorities had an administrative centre here and the Marché Neuf, built to replace Montréal's first market in Place Royale, was nearby. The present building was never meant to serve as a market. The British erected it between 1845 and 1850 to fill cultural and political needs: The city councillors met downstairs and singers and musicians entertained the elite in the concert hall upstairs. It was only in 1878, when the mayor and city legislators moved to their new home on rue Notre-Dame, that it became a market and remained so until the early 1960s. After a 1963 redevelopment, the building served again as municipal offices until May 1996, when it reopened as a shopping arcade full of boutiques.

Building The present grey stone building is one of the most graceful in the city. Its long neoclassical facade, punctuated by rows of white-painted sash windows, stretches for two city blocks. The main portico, supported by six cast-iron Doric columns moulded in England, fronts on cobbled rue Saint-Paul in the heart of the old city. The building is once again open to the public. Local artists and artisans display their wares in shops and stalls on the lower level and the upper floor is used for exhibits on Montréal's marine history, and for concerts and banquets. The back door of the Marché opens on the Vieux-Port (► 47). In summer there is an outdoor café at street level.

A landmark on the Montréal waterfront

Vieux-Port de Montréal

Montréal's old port has been transformed from a tangle of rusting rail lines and crumbling warehouses into one of the city's most popular parks, with bicycle trails, lawns, cafés, and a state-of-the-art science centre.

Seaways Although Montreal is nearly 1600km (1000mi) from the sea, its position at the confluence of the Ottawa and St. Lawrence rivers made it an important trading port—a gateway to the Great Lakes cities of Canada and the US and the fur- and mineral-rich territory of the northwest. The old harbour bustled until the 1970s, when huge container ships rendered it obsolete. Shipping operations moved downriver and the port sank into decay.

Instant hit Vieux-Port was popular from the day it opened as a park in 1992. In winter the February Fête des Neiges attracts thousands of revellers, and the huge skating rink is always in use. In summer the promenade along the waterfront is alive with skateboarders, strollers, cyclists, and street performers. You can hire bicycles, in-line skates and pedal-operated paddle boats. Private operators offer harbour cruises and jet-boat rides on the Lachine Rapids. A ferry takes foot passengers to the park on Île Sainte-Hélène (➤ 48). The King Edward Pier is the home of iSci, Montréal's innovative science centre. It combines education (interactive science displays, exhibits on technology, and two IMAX theatres), restaurants, and shopping (gift shop and outdoor market). At the eastern end of the port, visitors with good hearts can climb the 192 steps to the top of the Tour de l'Horloge—erected in memory of merchant mariners killed during World War I—for a fantastic view of the waterfront.

HIGHLIGHTS

- iSci
- Cinéma IMAX
- Jet boating
- La Tour de l'Horloge
- Harbour cruises
- People watching

INFORMATION

- ➕ G7; locator map F2
- ✉ Access across old rail tracks at points along rue de la Commune
- ☎ 514/496-PORT or 514/873-2015; www.oldportofmontreal.com
- 🕐 Varies with attraction
- 🍽 Place Jacques-Cartier, Maison des Écluisiers and Pointe-à-Callière
- Ⓜ Champ-des-Mars, Place-d'Armes, Square-Victoria
- 🚌 38, 55, 61, 129
- ♿ Good
- Ⓘ Free access to site. iSci expensive
- 🔄 Basilique Notre-Dame (➤ 40), Centre d'histoire de Montréal (➤ 41), Musée d'archéologie (➤ 42)
- ℹ Pavilion Jacques-Cartier, Quai Jacques-Cartier

Île Sainte-Hélène

Rustic calm meets urban energy on this lovely island in the middle of the St. Lawrence River. Its meadows and woodlands echo to the rattle of musket fire, the screams of roller-coaster riders, and the music of open-air concerts.

Top: at the David M. Stewart Museum
Above: Habitat '67

Island Two things transformed Île Sainte-Hélène from an isolated offshore green space into a vibrant city park: the building of the Jacques Cartier Bridge in 1930 between the island and the city; and Expo '67, which opened the island to the world. To prepare for it the city dumped tons of rubble from Métro excavations into the river to create space for pavilions, more than doubling the island's size.

Attractions One of the fair's signature buildings—the geodesic dome that was the American pavilion—now encloses the Biosphère, an environmental interpretive centre. Other Expo holdovers include La Ronde, the amusement park, now bigger and better than in 1967, and containing one of the world's biggest roller-coasters; an amphitheatre used for open-air concerts; and Alexander Calder's huge metal sculpture, *Man*. A man-made lake is the setting for a summer-long fireworks competition. On the Cité du Havre peninsula opposite the island is Moshe Safdie's block modular housing known as Habitat '67. One of the island's best attractions predates the fair by more than 100 years. The Old Fort was built by the British after the War of 1812. Its barracks house the David M. Stewart Museum and its parade square rattles to the musket drills of the Fraser Highlanders and the Compagnie Franche de la Marine—two 18th-century rivals now sharing one fort.

La Biosphère

There are two very good reasons for a visit to the Biosphère: to marvel at the shimmering geometric dome designed by Buckminster Fuller; and to see the centre's fascinating interactive displays about the environment.

Masterpiece The Biosphère is relatively new— it opened only in 1995—but it is framed by what is left of one of Expo '67's most enduring architectural landmarks. When Expo opened, the glittering sphere that housed the US pavilion was the world's biggest geodesic structure and one of the fair's most popular attractions. After- wards, it housed an aviary and was known as the world's largest bird cage. But in 1976 fire destroyed the dome's acrylic skin, reducing the proud structure to a corroding metal skeleton.

New role Displays inside now highlight the ecosystems of the Great Lakes and St. Lawrence River, a network of waterways that not only provides a vital lifeline for trade, but whose shores are also home to nearly half of Canada's population. Tours open in the Discovery Hall, where an eye-catching 5m (16ft) globe helps explain the importance of water to our daily lives. In the Visions Hall, you enjoy views of the river and the city, while in the Connections Hall models, computers, and diagrams demonstrate dramatically how we all share the same water as it falls as rain, runs through streams, is piped in and out of homes, and flows into the sea; you can also see the effect of pollution along the way. Take advantage of the soothing properties of water by bathing your feet (towels are provided).

HIGHLIGHTS

- River views
- Globe
- Water theatre
- Satellite-fed data
- Interactive displays

INFORMATION

- ➕ J6; locator map off E4
- ✉ 160 chemin du Tour-de-Île, Île Sainte-Hélène
- ☎ 514/283-5000; http://biosphere.ec.gc.ca/bio/
- 🕐 Late Jun–early Sep: daily 10–6. Early Sep–late Jun: Wed–Sun 10–5
- 🚇 Jean-Drapeau
- 🚌 167 Les Îles (in summer)
- ♿ Very good
- 💰 Moderate
- ↔ Île Sainte-Hélène (➤ 48), Île Notre-Dame (➤ 50)
- ❓ Guided tours

The Discovery Hall's globe

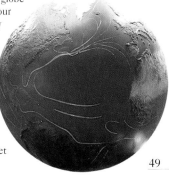

Île Notre-Dame

HIGHLIGHTS

- Beach
- Views
- Floral Park
- Casino

INFORMATION

- ✚ K7–J5; locator map off E4
- ✉ Île Notre-Dame Casino: 1 avenue du Casino
- ☎ Casino 514/392-2746 (or toll-free 800/665-2274 in Canada and the US). Beach 514/872-6211
- 🕓 Casino daily 24 hours. Beach 23 Jun–27 Aug: daily 10–7 (if fine)
- 🚇 Jean-Drapeau
- 🚌 167 Les Îles (summer)
- ⛴ Summer ferry from Bassin Jacques-Cartier
- ♿ Variable
- 💰 Casino free. Beach moderate
- ↔ Île Ste-Hélène (➤ 48), La Biosphère (➤ 49)
- ❓ Casino: visitors must be over 18; the wearing of shorts, leggings, T-shirts, sportwear, beachwear, running shoes, and denim of any kind is not allowed

The popular Casino de Montréal

Before Expo '67, this long thin island hugging the south shore of the St. Lawrence River didn't exist. Today it offers a huge variety of activities—car racing, swimming, and gambling—in addition to some magnificent views of the Montréal skyline.

Engineering When you bore a subway system through solid granite, you have to find somewhere to put all the rock you excavate. In the giddy days of the early 1960s Montréal's visionary mayor Jean Drapeau decided to drop it in the middle of the St. Lawrence River to create the venue for a world fair. He doubled the size of Île Sainte-Hélène (➤ 48), and created a brand new island right next to it. Now the two islands form one park, and when Drapeau died in 1999 the city named it Parc Jean-Drapeau.

Attractions The most popular attraction on the island, and one of the most popular in the city, is the Casino de Montréal. Its owner, the Québec provincial government, has tried to recreate the glamour of a European gambling palace in two spectacular buildings, the former French and Québec Expo '67 pavilions. Apart from its 3,000 slot machines and 118 gaming tables, the casino also houses five restaurants and a cabaret. The island's second-most popular attraction is the beach on the man-made lake. The only one within the city limits, it is kept clean by a unique filtration system that uses aquatic plants. The island is also home to the Circuit Gilles-Villeneuve, the only Formula 1 racing track in North America and home of the Air Canada Grand Prix. A vast floral park, built for the Floralies Internationales festival in 1980, it is laced with canals and waterways, and filled with flowers, rose bushes, and trees.

MONTRÉAL's
best

Museums & Galleries

History comes to life at the David M. Stewart Museum

MUSEUM PASS

La Carte-Musées Montréal
☎ 514/845-6873 offers free
admission to 19 of the city's
leading museums including all
those on these pages as well
as all the sights and museums
in the Top 25 Sights (except for
those on pages 26–28).

┌─ **In the Top 25** ─
CANADIAN CENTRE FOR ARCHITECTURE (▶ 34)
CENTRE D'HISTOIRE DE MONTRÉAL (▶ 41)
MCCORD MUSEUM (▶ 32)
**MUSÉE D'ARCHÉOLOGIE ET D'HISTOIRE DE LA
   POINTE-À-CALLIÈRE (▶ 42)**
MUSÉE D'ART CONTEMPORAIN (▶ 38)
MUSÉE DES BEAUX-ARTS (▶ 33)

CHÂTEAU DUFRESNE

The sumptuous interiors of these magnificent Beaux
Arts homes, built in 1918 by Mario and Oscar
Dufresne, offer a glimpse into the life of Montréal's
French-speaking haute bourgeoisie.
✚ G12 ✉ 2929 avenue Jeanne-d'Arc ☎ 514/259-9201
🕐 Thu–Sun 10–5 🚇 Pie-IX 🅰 Good 💰 Moderate

DAVID M. STEWART MUSEUM

Home to collections of firearms, maps, scientific
instruments, and domestic artefacts. Look in
particular for the 18th-century kitchen.
✚ H5 ✉ Le Fort, Île Sainte-Hélène ☎ 514/861-6701
🕐 Mid-May to early Sep: daily 10–6. Early Sep to mid-May: Wed–Mon
10–5 🚇 Île Sainte-Hélène 🚌 167 🅰 Poor 💰 Moderate

ÉCOMUSÉE DU FIER MONDE

Photographs and period artefacts are used to illustrate
the Industrial Revolution and its impact on Montréal
and its people.
✚ F5 ✉ 2050 rue Amherst ☎ 514/528-8444;

www.ecomusee.qc.ca 🖰 Wed 11–8; Thu–Fri 9.30–4; Sat–Sun 10.30–5
🚇 Sherbrooke, Berri 🚌 24 🖖 Good 🎫 Moderate

MUSÉE JUSTE POUR RIRE
Film clips, stage sets, cartoons, and costumes are
used to trace the history of comedy. The museum
also has a video café and performance space.
🖰 F6 ✉ 2111 boulevard Saint-Laurent ☎ 514/845-4000
🖰 Early Jun–early Sep: daily 11–8. Rest of the year: call for times
🍴 Café 🚇 Saint-Laurent 🚌 24, 55

MUSÉE MARC-AURÈLE FORTIN
Self-taught Québec artist Marc-Aurèle Fortin
(1888–1970) set out to create a whole new style of
landscape painting, and was particularly fond of
painting massive trees. Fortin also experimented with
painting on grey or black backgrounds. This is the
only museum dedicated to the work of one artist,
though it sometimes shows work by other Québécois.
🖰 G7 ✉ 118 rue Saint-Pierre ☎ 514/845-6108 🖰 Tue–Sun
11–5 🚇 Square-Victoria (exit rue Saint-Jacques) 🚌 61 (57 peak
hours) 🖖 Poor: eight steps to main entrance 🎫 Moderate

MUSÉE DES HOSPITALIÈRES
This museum tells the story of Hôtel-Dieu,
Montréal's first hospital, and
the Hospitalières de Saint-
Joseph, recruited in France
in 1659 by Montréal's
co-founder, Jeanne Mance;
the collection captures
something of the religious
fervour of the age.
🖰 E6 ✉ 201 avenue des Pins Ouest
☎ 514/849-2919 🖰 Mid-Jun to
mid-Oct: Tue–Fri 10–5; Sat, Sun 1–5.
Mid-Oct to mid-Jun: Wed–Sun 1–5
🚇 Sherbrooke 🚌 144 🖖 Fair
🎫 Moderate

MAISON DE LA POSTE
The only philatelic centre in Canada devoted entirely
to the sale of Canadian stamps.
🖰 F8 ✉ 1250 rue Université ☎ 514/846-5401 🖰 Mon–Fri
9–5.45 🚇 McGill 🚌 107 🖖 Good 🎫 Free

MAISON SAINT-GABRIEL
Saint Marguerite Bourgeoys ran a farm and school
from this fine 17th-century farmhouse, still standing
among the tenements of Pointe-Saint-Charles. The
house is full of artefacts from the period.
🖰 G10 ✉ 2146 Place Dublin ☎ 514/935-8136 🖰 Mid-Apr to
mid-Dec: daily 9–5 🚇 Charlevoix 🚌 57 🖖 Good 🎫 Moderate

LE MONDE DE MAURICE RICHARD
No one played ice hockey
more passionately than
Maurice (Rocket) Richard who
wore a Canadiens uniform
from 1944 to 1960. He was the
first player to score 50 goals in
a season (which at that time
was only 50 games long). This
tiny museum pays him
homage with pictures, jerseys,
pucks, and other artefacts.
🖰 G1 ✉ 2800 rue Viau
☎ 514/251-9930 🖰 Tue–Sun
11–5 🚇 Viau 🖖 Good
🎫 Free

Inspirational ice hockey player Maurice Richard

Squares

NELSON'S COLUMN

It seems odd that the statue of an English admiral should grace a square named for French explorer Jacques Cartier. Odder still that it should be French-speaking Sulpician priests who led the campaign to raise the monument to Horatio Nelson after his victory over a Franco-Spanish fleet in 1805 in the Napoleonic Wars. The priests were anxious to show they were good subjects, and had little sympathy for the agnostic Corsican emperor.

PLACE D'ARMES

Place d'Armes was laid out at the end of the 17th century around the "Gadoys" well, the main source of drinking water for Montréal's first French settlement. In the centre stands a statue (1895) of Paul de Chomedey, Montréal's founder, Sieur de Maisonneuve, who is supposed to have killed an Iroquois chieftain on this spot in 1644. Around it lie the Basilique Notre-Dame (▶ 40), Séminaire St-Sulpice (▶ 56), the Banque de Montréal (▶ 56), the 1930 art deco Aldred Building, or Édifice Prevoyance (▶ 57), and the eight-storey Édifice New York Life (1888). To the south is the waterfront and Vieux-Port attractions (▶ 47).

➕ G7 🚇 Place d'Armes

SQUARE PHILLIPS

An immense, pigeon-spattered statue of King Edward VII, sculpted by Philippe Hébert in 1914, dominates this pleasant open space on rue Sainte-Catherine in the middle of downtown. In summer street vendors open stands at the king's feet, competing with the shops that surround the square. Across the street and slightly to the west is Christ Church Cathedral (▶ 35).

➕ F7 🚇 McGill

PLACE JACQUES-CARTIER

Right in the heart of Vieux-Montréal, this lovely cobbled square was created in 1804 as a municipal market; now its cafés, musicians, restaurants, and quaint shops draw lively summer crowds. Nelson's Column (see panel) stands here and there are several fine 19th-century houses, including Maison del Vecchio, Maison Cartier, and Maison Vandelac.

➕ G7
🚇 Champ-de-Mars

Nelson's Column, overlooking Place Jacques-Cartier

PLACE ROYALE

The city's oldest public square was formerly used as both a market and meeting place between French settlers and native peoples. It was later the site of duels, whippings, and public hangings.

➕ G7
🚇 Place-d'Armes

PLACE D'YOUVILLE

This Vieux-Port square, very pleasant when not full of cars, was landscaped over a dried-up creek during the 19th century, which is the reason for its strange shape. It housed a fish market at one stage, and was used by people meeting ships moored nearby.

➕ G7 🚇 Square-Victoria

SQUARE-DORCHESTER

This major downtown green space is lined with churches, historic buildings, and office buildings. Just off rue Sainte-Catherine—the city's main shopping street—it's popular in summer with visitors and city workers alike. The main Infotouriste tourist office is here.

➕ F7–F8 🚇 Peel, Bonaventure

SQUARE SAINT-LOUIS

This leafy square was laid out in 1879, away from downtown and the Vieux-Port, and is considered one of the city's finest. Its beautiful houses—formerly owned by Montréal's mercantile elite—are now home to poets, artists, and writers attracted by the Bohemian atmosphere of the surrounding Saint-Denis district. At its southern end lies the pedestrians-only rue Prince-Arthur Est, full of street entertainers in summer.

➕ F6 🚇 Sherbrooke

Elegant Victorian houses in Square Saint-Louis

THE FAUBOURGS

Originally built almost entirely of wood, Montréal was constantly devastated by fires. Edicts in 1721 and 1727 made stone construction mandatory within the city walls. Those who could not afford stone began to build outside the city walls, thus creating Montréal's four "faubourgs" (suburbs)— Saint-Laurent, Québec, Récollets, and Saint-Louis. Here the houses had foundations and fireplaces of stone, but used timber for the walls and roofs.

Historic Buildings

The ornate interior of the
Banque de Montréal

BANQUE DE MONTRÉAL

The Bank of Montréal, Canada's oldest
financial institution, was founded in 1817.
Thirty years later its headquarters moved to
this neoclassical building inspired by Rome's
Pantheon. The bank has a small museum
displaying coins, mechanical piggy banks,
and a cheque written on a beaver pelt.

➕ G7 ✉ 119 rue Saint-Jacques ☎ 514/877-6892
🕐 Mon–Fri 10–4 🚇 Place-d'Armes ♿ Good
💰 Free

MAISON PAPINEAU

This beautifully restored 18th-century
building was home to Louis-Joseph Papineau
(1786–1871), who played a leading role in the
French-Canadian nationalist movement until
the rebellion of 1837. Note the house's steep
roof, designed to prevent the build-up of
snow, and the facade, much of which appears
to be rusticated (cut) stone but is actually
cleverly carved wood.

➕ G6 ✉ 440 rue Bonsecours ☎ None 🕐 Exterior only
🚇 Champ-de-Mars ♿ On a sloping, cobbled street

OLDEST BUILDING

Montréal's oldest building is
the Séminaire Saint-Sulpice,
closed to the public but visible
through the gate to the west of
the Basilique Notre-Dame
(► 40). It was built in 1685
for the Sulpicians, a Paris-
based order of priests, who
were proprietors of the entire
island of Montréal and who
planned and named many of
the city's streets and squares.
The clock (1710) over the main
entrance is reputedly North
America's oldest timepiece.

MAISON PIERRE-DU-CALVET

This fine 18th-century house was built in 1770 for
Huguenot merchant Pierre du Calvet, who was
notorious for switching allegiance between the
French, British, and Americans as each controlled
Montréal. Note the thick walls and fireplaces, the
windows with little squares of glass imported from
France, and the S-shape brackets on the facade, the
only visible part of the bars used to strengthen the
internal wooden beams of the building.

➕ G6 ✉ 401 rue Bonsecours ☎ 514/282-1725
🚇 Champ-de-Mars

VIEUX PALAIS DE JUSTICE

This impressive neoclassical courthouse, built in
1856, was used for almost a century to hear civil
cases. Most of it is now used for municipal offices, but
you can still admire the dome, exterior columns, and
impressive portico.

➕ G7 ✉ 155 rue Notre-Dame Est 🚇 Champ-de-Mars

Modern Architecture

ÉDIFICE IBM-MARATHON

Designed in 1991 by New York's Kohn, Pederson, Fox, this 47-storey glass-and-granite tower is one of Montréal's most innovative.

➕ F8 ✉ 1250 boulevard René-Lévesque Ouest between rues Stanley and Drummond 🚇 Bonaventure

HABITAT '67

This angular 100-apartment complex was designed for Expo '67 by Moshe Safdie, one of the city's leading architects. The apartments are now some of the city's most sought after.

➕ H7–H8 ✉ Avenue Pierre-Dupuy, Cité du Havre 🚇 Place d'Armes ❓ Clearly visible from the Vieux-Port and Pointe-à-Callière

MAISON ALCAN

The Aluminum Company of Canada headquarters designed by Montréal architect Rag Affleck (1983) blends old and new and has a stunning atrium.

➕ E7 ✉ 1188 rue Sherbrooke Ouest ☎ 514/848-8000 ♿ Very good 🚇 Peel ❓ Guided tours. Free lunch-time foyer concerts

PLACE VILLE-MARIE

This cruciform aluminium tower designed by I. M. Pei (completed in 1962) was Montréal's first modern skyscraper. Its vast plaza is popular in summer and its street-level mall was the first element of the Underground City (► 36).

➕ F7 ✉ Boulevard René-Lévesque between rues Mansfield and University 🚇 Bonaventure/McGill

TOUR BNP-BANQUE LAURENTIENNE

These twin blue-glass towers are eye-catching on the downtown skyline, dominating a particularly pleasant stretch of avenue McGill.

➕ E7 ✉ 1981 avenue McGill College 🚇 McGill

WESTMOUNT SQUARE

This black-metal and tinted-glass masterpiece by the eminent modernist architect Ludwig Mies van der Rohe dates from 1964.

➕ D9 ✉ Rue Sainte-Catherine Ouest at avenue Greene 🚇 Atwater

MIDDLE-AGED

Fine Montréal buildings that are considered neither old nor new include the monolithic Édifice Sun Life (1914), reputed for many years to be the British Empire's largest building (✉ 1155 rue Metcalfe), and the Romanesque Windsor Station (1889), the former headquarters of the Canadian Pacific Railway (✉ Corner of rues Peel and de la Gauchetière).

The innovative Édifice IBM-Marathon (right)

ART DECO

The Aldred Building, or Édifice Prevoyance (1928), is celebrated for its interesting art deco features (✉ 501–507 Place d'Armes). Édifice Ernest Cormier (1930), a grand neoclassical former courthouse, is now a centre for the performing arts (✉ 100 rue Notre-Dame Est).

Green Spaces

VIEWPOINTS

For the best views, go to the Chalet terrace or the East Side Lookout off the Voie Camilien-Houde, both in the Parc du Mont-Royal (► 29); the Oratoire Saint-Joseph, at the city's highest point (► 30); the little observatory in the Chapelle Notre-Dame-de-Bonsecours (► 45); or ride on the exciting tramway up the Olympic Stadium's famous tower (► 27).

PARC ANGRIGNON

This park has a small working farm, La Petite Ferme Angrignon, with guided tours and educational activities.

🔲 Off map at A13 ✉ 3400 boulevard des Trinitaires ☎ 514/872-3816; La Petite Ferme Angrignon 514/872-1400 ⏰ Park daily dawn to dusk. La Petite Ferme Angrignon early Jun–early Sep: daily 9–5 Ⓜ Angrignon ♿ Good 🎟 Free

PARC LAFONTAINE

Lafontaine divides into an English-style landscape in the west and a French-style garden in the east, with tennis courts, outdoor swimming pools, and summer concerts.

🔲 F4–F5 ✉ Rue Sherbrooke Est between rue Saint-Hubert and avenue Papineau ⏰ Daily 9AM–10PM 🍴 Snack bar Ⓜ Sherbrooke (eight-block walk) ♿ Good 🎟 Free

PARC MAISONNEUVE

Parc Maisonneuve's slopes and frozen lakes are ideal for tobogganing, cross-country skiing, and skating. You can picnic, walk, cycle, and play golf in summer.

🔲 F1–G1 ✉ 4601 rue Sherbrooke Est and boulevard Pie-XI ☎ 514/872-6555 ⏰ Daily 9AM–10PM Ⓜ Viau, Pie-IX ♿ Good 🎟 Park free. Golf course moderate

PARC WESTMOUNT

Said to be the loveliest city park, Westmount contains playing fields, a conservatory, and a stellar playground.

🔲 D9–D10 ✉ Rue Sherbrooke Ouest between avenues Landsdowne and Melville ☎ None ⏰ Park daily 9AM–dusk. Conservatory usually daily 9–3 🍴 Cafés nearby Ⓜ Place Saint-Henri, Vendôme ♿ Good

Parc Lafontaine

Streets & Boulevards

RUE BONSECOURS
A good example of the classical ideals of Montréal's early French planners, with fine homes. Look for No. 401 Maison Pierre-du-Calvet and No. 440 Maison Papineau (both ➤ 56).
🚹 G6 🚇 Champ-de-Mars

AVENUE MCGILL COLLEGE
This short wide boulevard runs from Cathcart near Place Ville-Marie up to McGill University's Roddick Gates. If you stand on the Place Ville-Marie plaza, you get a beautiful sweeping view of the mountains and the campus framed by glass office towers.
🚹 E7–F7 🚇 McGill

The bright lights of rue Sainte-Catherine

RUE SAINT-AMABLE
This narrow and lively cobbled alley off Place Jacques-Cartier is notorious for the many portrait artists vying for business amid the summer throng.
🚹 G7 🚇 Place-d'Armes

RUE SAINTE-CATHERINE
Montréal's premier shopping street, spoiled in places by fast-food joints, is at its best between rues University and Peel, and within the area of rues de la Montagne, Crescent, and Bishop.
🚹 E8–F7 🚇 Guy-Concordia

RUE SAINT-DENIS
Rue Saint-Denis bisects Montréal's Quartier Latin, a slightly seedy area that is now being filled with interesting cafés, bistros, and shops.
🚹 F6–G6 🚇 Berri-UQAM, Sherbrooke

RUE SAINT-PAUL
A block back from the waterfront, this is one of the city's oldest and most fashionable streets, with rather expensive cafés, restaurants, and fascinating specialist shops.
🚹 G6–G8 🚇 Place-d'Armes, Champ-de-Mars

RUE SHERBROOKE
The most interesting section of this major street flanks an area whose residents were once estimated to own 70 percent of Canada's wealth. You can still find luxury shops, hotels, and galleries.
🚹 E7–E8 🚇 Peel, McGill

THE MAIN

Boulevard Saint-Laurent, or The Main, still officially marks the division between west and east in the city. It housed Montréal's earliest immigrants and today has an incredibly varied ethnic and cultural mix. Its surrounding streets are full of bookstores, bric-a-brac stores, second-hand clothes shops and interesting bars, bistros, and restaurants.

59

Children's Activities

The Planétarium de Montréal, popular for its shows on the solar system

JUST FOR KIDS

Most of the major city museums have special activity schedules for children. The Musée des beaux-arts (➤ 33) offers hands-on creative sessions on Sunday mornings. The Canadian Centre for Architecture (➤ 34) has weekend toy-making workshops. The Redpath Museum at McGill University (➤ 31) has Sunday workshops to introduce children to science.

In the Top 25

BIODÔME (➤ 26)
BIOSPHÈRE (➤ 49)
ÎLE NOTRE-DAME (➤ 50)
ÎLE SAINTE-HÉLÈNE (➤ 48)
PARC OLYMPIQUE (➤ 27)

CIRQUE DU SOLEIL (➤ 82)

COSMODOME

The adventure of space exploration is the focus of this centre in surburban Laval, a 30-minute drive from downtown. It's affiliated with the US Space Camp Foundation and is loaded with such kid-pleasing exhibits as replicas of rockets and space ships, and a full-size mock-up of the space shuttle Endeavor. There are films—some of them shown on a 360-degree screen—as well as games and demonstrations.
➕ Off map at A3 ✉ 2150 Autoroute de Laurentides, Laval
☎ 514/978-3615 or 800/565-CAMP 🕐 24 Jun–1 Sep: daily 10–6.
2 Sep–23 Jun: Tue–Sun 10–6 💵 Expensive

LABYRINTHE DU HANGAR 16

This weather-protected maze in the Vieux-Port has a new theme every year. Route and clues change periodically with new obstacles, traps, and play zones.
➕ G6 ✉ Quai de L'Horloge, Vieux-Port ☎ 514/400-0099
🕐 18 May–21 Jun, 26 Aug–29 Sep: daily 11.30–5.30. 22 Jun–25 Aug: 11–9 🚇 Champ-de-Mars 💵 Moderate

PLANÉTARIUM DE MONTRÉAL

Regular shows in the big domed theatre offer guided tours to our solar system and more distant galaxies. Themed schedules alter every few months, exploring space collisions, black holes, sun spots, eclipses, and the star that guided the Magi to Bethlehem.
➕ F8 ✉ 1000 rue Saint-Jacques Ouest ☎ 514/872-4530
🕐 24 Jun–2 Sep: daily. 3 Sep–2 Jun: Tue–Sun 💵 Moderate

Free Attractions

PARKS

Look for free concerts in summer in Montréal's parks (► 58). In the Parc du Mont-Royal, you can enjoy great views of downtown and listen to the Montréal Symphony Orchestra's summer performances alongside Lac-aux-Castors (Beaver Lake). The Île Sainte-Hélène and Île Notre-Dame (► 48, 50) are also lively in summer.

MUSEUMS

Several of the city's larger museums have one free late-evening admittance each week. At press time there is no charge for the McCord Museum from 6PM to 9PM on Thursdays (► 32), or for the permanent collection at the Musée des beaux-arts (► 33), while the main collection of the Musée d'art contemporain is free on Wednesdays from 6PM to 9PM and for some weekend sessions (► 38). There is no charge for The Banque du Montréal (► 56), the Maison de la Poste (► 53), and the Redpath Museum (► 31).

CONCERTS AND FESTIVALS

The Oratoire Saint-Joseph (► 30) has free organ recitals on Wednesday evenings in summer and carillon concerts from Wednesday to Saturday year-round. The atrium of the Maison Alcan (► 57) regularly hosts free lunch-time concerts. Admission to midday and evening organ and choral concerts in Christ Church Cathedral is by donation. The famous Jazz and Juste Pour Rire festivals (► 10) have many outdoor shows open to all. Free concerts take place at the Vieux-Port in summer and there is an open-air theatre in Parc Lafontaine (► 58).

FREE AND ALMOST FREE

Watch the world go by in an open-air café, amble around the Vieux-Port, linger with the night-time crowds on rues Sainte-Catherine Ouest and Saint-Denis, or try the multiethnic shops and markets of The Main (► 30) on a Saturday morning. To enjoy street performers, head for the Vieux-Port or the pedestrianized rue Prince-Arthur Est.

People-watching is one of Montréal's favourite free entertainments

On the River

CRUISE FOR LESS

In summer, the ferry trip from the Vieux-Port to Longueuil across the St. Lawrence makes a great quick getaway on the water—and the price is right. The boat stops at La Rondae on Île Sainte-Hélène. Frequencies vary, but it runs hourly from 10AM to 1AM in each direction in July and August. ➕ G7 ✉ Departs Quai Jacques-Cartier ☎ 514/281-8000 🕐 Mid-May to mid-Oct

Croisières Nouvelle-Orléans paddle steamer

BATEAU-MOUCHE

Take a trip on this glass-topped boat that explores the St. Lawrence and its islands. Le Canard Malard, a large inflatable operated by the same company, offers ecological and historical trips.
➕ G7 ✉ Quai Jacques-Cartier 🚢 Bateau Mouche 514/849-9952 (toll-free 800/361-9952 in Canada and the US). Le Canard Malard 514/285-8848 or 514/565-5815 🕐 Early May–early Oct: daily at 10, 12, 2, 4; dinner cruise at 7PM. Le Canard Malard: Île Grosbois daily at 10, 1, 4; sunset cruise at 7PM 🚇 Champ-de-Mars ♿ Good 💰 Expensive

CROISIÈRES NOUVELLE-ORLÉANS

Cruise the St. Lawrence and islands aboard a Mississippi-style paddle steamer.
➕ G7 ✉ Quai Jacques-Cartier ☎ 514/842-7655 (toll-free 1-800/667-3131 in Canada and the US) 🕐 Cruises mid-May to mid-Oct: daily at 12, 2, and 4; dinner-dance cruise 7PM 🚇 Champ-de-Mars ♿ Good 💰 Expensive

CROISIÈRES DÉCOUVERTES DU PORT

Take a 2-hour cruise, a dinner-dance cruise around Montréal, or a day trip to the Îles de Sorel, 48km (30mi) down river.
➕ H6 ✉ Quai de l'Horloge at rue Bonsecours ☎ 514/842-3871 (toll-free 1-800/667-3131 in Canada and the US) 🕐 Island Discovery mid-May to mid-Oct: daily at 12, 2.30. Îles de Sorel mid-Jun to early Sep: daily at 8AM 🚇 Champ-de-Mars ♿ Good 💰 Expensive

SAUTE-MOUTONS

Shoot the Lachine Rapids aboard open hydrofoil-type boats or by speedboat.
➕ G7 ✉ Office: 105 rue de la Commune. Departures: Saute-Moutons at Quai de L'Horloge; Jet Saint-Laurent at Quai Jacques-Cartier ☎ 514/284-9607 🕐 Saute-Moutons May–Sep: daily every 2 hours 10–6. Jet Saint-Laurent May–Sep: daily every 30 minutes 10–7 🚇 Champ-de-Mars ♿ Very good 💰 Expensive. Reservations required; no children under 6 years

MONTRÉAL
where to...

French

PRICES

Expect to pay for a meal per person, excluding drinks, service charge, and federal and provincial taxes (which amount to just over 15 percent):

$	under $20
$$	$20–$40
$$$	more than $40

À LA DÉCOUVERTE ($$)

Classic French cuisine on a quiet residential street in the Plateau Mont-Royal. Reserve two weeks in advance for weekends. BYOB.

🕂 E4 ✉ 4350 rue de la Roche ☎ 514/529-8377 🕔 Wed–Sat dinner 🚇 Mont-Royal 🛈 Reservations essential

AU BISTRO GOURMET ($$)

Classic bistro food: mussels in pullet sauce, kidney in dijonaise sauce, pear *trottoir*.

🕂 E8 ✉ 2100 rue Saint-Mathieu ☎ 514/846-1553 🕔 Mon–Fri lunch, dinner; Sat, Sun dinner

BISTRO L'ENTREPONT ($$)

Widely considered the best BYOB, perfect for a romantic French dinner. Dress up.

🕂 D5 ✉ 4622 avenue de l'Hotel-de-Ville ☎ 514/845-1369 🕔 Daily dinner (Sat: two sittings at 6 and 9) 🚇 Mont-Royal 🛈 Reservations essential

BONAPARTE ($$$)

Sit in the fireplace room overlooking rue Saint-Sacrement and you'll swear you're in Paris.

🕂 G7 ✉ 443 rue Saint-François-Xavier ☎ 514/844-4368 🕔 Mon–Fri lunch, dinner; Sat, Sun dinner 🚇 Place d'Armes 🛈 Reservations in summer

BORIS BISTRO ($$)

Bistro food—homemade sausage, braised rabbit—with a lighter touch served on a magnificent terrace in Vieux-Montréal. Perfect for lunch.

🕂 G7 ✉ 443 rue McGill ☎ 514/848-9575;

www.borisbistro.com 🕔 Daily lunch, dinner 🚇 Square Victoria 🛈 Reservations recommended

LE CAVEAU ($$)

French cooking in a three-storey town house. The upper levels are airier.

🕂 E7 ✉ 2063 rue Victoria between rue Sherbooke Ouest and avenue du Président-Kennedy ☎ 514/844-1624 🕔 Mon–Fri lunch, dinner; Sat, Sun dinner 🚇 McGill 🛈 Reservations

LES CAPRICES DE NICHOLAS ($$$)

The atrium garden of this prettily decorated, three-room restaurant is the perfect place for truffle-scented warm quail and spinach salad.

🕂 E8 ✉ 2072 rue Drummond ☎ 514/282-9790 🕔 Daily lunch, dinner 🚇 Peel 🛈 Reservations required

CHEZ LA MÈRE MICHEL ($$$)

Conservative but perfect dishes—lobster soufflé Mantua, bison, and caribou in season—at this well known downtown restaurant.

🕂 E8 ✉ 1209 rue Guy ☎ 514/934-0473 🕔 Daily lunch, dinner 🚇 Guy/Concordia 🛈 Reservations recommended

LA LOUX ($$)

Classic French food with a modern edge in a discreet, elegant setting.

🕂 E6 ✉ 250 avenue des Pins Est ☎ 514/287-9127 🕔 Mon–Fri lunch, dinner; Sat, Sun dinner 🚇 Sherbooke 🛈 Reservations recommended

LE MAS DES OLIVIERS ($$$)

Chef-owner Jacques

Muller fills his clients' plates with such deeply satisfying dishes as lamb loin with marrow in port sauce, and quail in puff pastry. And the *pescadou et sa rouquine*, an aromatic fish soup, is superb.

✚ E8 ⊠ 1216 rue Bishop ☎ 514/861-6733 🕐 Mon–Fri lunch, dinner; Sat, Sun dinner 🚇 Guy-Concordia ❓ Reservations recommended

NUANCES ($$$)

The Casino de Montréal's premier restaurant on Île Notre-Dame has glorious views of the city and a highly innovative menu featuring such signature dishes as loin of lamb cooked in clay served with gnocchi in an oregano oil.

✚ J7 ⊠ 1 avenue de Casino, Île Notre-Dame ☎ 514/392-2708 🕐 Mon–Sat lunch, dinner; Sun dinner 🚇 Guy-Concordia ❓ Reservations recommended

LE PARIS ($$)

This downtown restaurant has been serving such comfort dishes as grilled blood pudding, cod *brandade* and calf's liver *neunière* since 1956.

✚ E8 ⊠ 1812 rue Sainte-Catherine Ouest ☎ 514/937-4898 🕐 Mon–Sat lunch, dinner; Sun dinner 🚇 Guy-Concordia ❓ Reservations recommended

LE PASSE PARTOUT ($$$)

New York-born chef James MacGuire makes the trek out to this West End restaurant well worthwhile. He bakes the best bread in Montréal.

✚ B10 ⊠ 3857 boulevard Décarie ☎ 514/487-7750 🕐 Thu, Fri lunch, dinner; Sat

dinner 🚇 Villa Maria ❓ Reservations essential

LE PÉGASE ($$)

Unpretentious neighbourhood place—try calf brains with spinach and almonds, or caribou chop with sun-dried tomatoes. BYOB.

✚ G5 ⊠ 1831 rue Gilford ☎ 514/522-0487 🕐 Tue–Sun dinner 🚇 Laurier/Mont-Royal 🚌 45 ❓ Reservations recommended

LES HALLES ($$$)

Long wine list, classic French cuisine. Less formal bistro.

✚ E8 ⊠ 1450 rue Crescent ☎ 514/844-2328 🕐 Tue–Fri lunch, dinner; Mon, Sat dinner 🚇 Peel ❓ Reservations recommended

LES REMPARTS ($$$)

The subtle lighting in this cellar restaurant creates a romantic atmosphere.

✚ G7 ⊠ 93 rue de la Commune Est ☎ 514/392-1649 🕐 Mon–Fri lunch, dinner; Sat, Sun dinner 🚇 Place d'Armes ❓ Reservations recommended

L'EXPRESS ($$)

Elbow-to-elbow tables, cheerfully frantic service, perfect food, and interesting wines.

✚ E5 ⊠ 3927 rue Saint-Denis at rue Duluth ☎ 514/845-5333 🕐 Daily lunch, dinner 🚇 Sherbrooke ❓ Reservations required

RESTAURANT JULIEN ($$$)

Fashionable downtown restaurant with a canopied terrace in summer.

✚ F7 ⊠ 1191 rue Union ☎ 514/871-1581 🕐 Mon–Fri lunch, dinner; Sat dinner

BRING YOUR OWN BOTTLE

If you are watching your budget, consider dining at a restaurant that allows you to bring your own wine. Entries are designated as "BYOB"—bring your own bottle (*Apporter son vin*). BYOB restaurants are common in Montréal, thanks to a quirk in Québec's provincial liquor laws. The food quality in these places ranges from pedestrian to excellent, but they are usually inexpensive. The restaurants sell no alcohol themselves, but they will gladly open your wine or beer and provide glasses. BYOBs first sprang up on rue Prince-Arthur Est, and spread to the streets around rue Duluth. Better places, however, can be found around rue Mentana and around avenues Mont-Royal and Marie-Anne, and in the Gay Village (Le Village) around rues Amherst and Ontario. Inexpensive wine can be bought at neighbourhood convenience stores (*dépanneurs*). Better wine is available at outlets of the Société des Alcools du Québec.

Eclectic & Contemporary

ETHNIC FLAVOURS

French cuisine in all its forms—provincial, bourgeois, classic, and updated—dominates Montréal's dining scene, although contemporary fusion fare, which draws on many ethnic flavours, has not taken hold as it has in California and New York. More than 30 different ethnic groups are represented in Montréal. The Greek and Italian immigrants who poured into the city in the latter half of the 20th century have established an enduring place in Montréalers' stomachs. Cantonese cooking has been a presence since Chinese railway workers established a foothold in the city in the late 1800s. Refugees from Indochina, who began arriving in the city in the late 1970s, opened Vietnamese restaurants and noodle shops. The current craze is for Thai food.

AREA ($$)

Opening dishes at this establishment in the heart of the Gay Village are exquisite—curried tempura tiger prawns, with a cool pepper/mango salsa, and perhaps best of all, deep-fried sweetbreads in a gingerbread-crumb crust served with a hot quince dipping jelly.
➕ G6 ✉ 1429 rue Amherst ☎ 514/890-6691 🕐 Tue–Fri lunch, dinner; Sat, Sun dinner 🚇 Beaudry ❓ Reservations essential

BAZOU ($$)

The name means "jalopy," a car theme reflected in the bright red and blue decor, and the names of the dishes; the duo Maserati, for example, is cannelloni with four meats and sauce napolitaine. Desserts are particularly good.
➕ F6 ✉ 2004 Hôtel-de-Ville ☎ 514/982-0853 🕐 Tue–Sat dinner 🚇 Saint-Laurent ❓ Reservations recommended

CUBE ($$$)

Super trendy restaurant in the boutique Hôtel Saint-Paul on the edge of Vieux-Montréal serves bold, market cuisine. Minimalist decor. Fashionable crowd.
➕ G7 ✉ 355 rue McGill ☎ 514/876-2823 🕐 Mon–Fri lunch, dinner; Sat, Sun dinner 🚇 Square Victoria ❓ Reservations required

CHEZ L'ÉPICIER ($$$)

Fresh market cuisine served in the surroundings of an old grocery store. Try the sweetbreads braised in apple juice and fresh thyme, or the salmon stew with salsify. Takeaway meals available.
➕ G7 ✉ 311 rue Saint-Paul ☎ 514/878-2232 🕐 Daily lunch, dinner 🚇 Champ-de-Mars ❓ Reservations recommended

LA CHRONIQUE ($$$)

No one blends the flavours of Europe, America, and Asia as seamlessly as chef Marc de Cank in dishes such as bok choy sweetbreads and wild-mushroom salsa. Pecan pie with Jack Daniel's and passion fruit soufflé are worth saving room for.
➕ D5 ✉ 99 avenue Laurier Ouest ☎ 514/271-3095 🕐 Tue–Sat dinner 🚇 Laurier 🚌 51

GLOBE ($$$)

The sleek, trendy decor is not as daring as the cooking—note the Québec foie gras pot-roasted with plum wine.
➕ F6 ✉ 3455 boulevard Saint-Laurent ☎ 514/284-3823 🕐 Daily dinner 🚇 Saint-Laurent 🚌 55

TOQUÉ! ($$$)

Chef-owner Normand Laprise's restaurant has been Montréal's undisputed temple of haute cuisine since the 1980s. Try such dishes as Cap-Saint Ignace quail with raspberry sauce, and roasted deer haunch with juniper berries. Vast wine cellar.
➕ E5 ✉ 3442 rue Saint-Denis ☎ 514/499-2084; www.restaurant-toque.com 🕐 Daily dinner 🚇 Sherbrooke ❓ Reservations required

Italian & Greek

DA EMMA ($$)
Stone-walled basement room near the Vieux-Port. Try the fettucine with porcini mushrooms or roast baby pig. Helpful service.

➕ G7 ✉ 777 rue de la Commune Ouest ☎ 514/392-568 🕐 Mon–Fri lunch, dinner; Sat dinner 🚇 Square Victoria ❓ Reservations for dinner

LA FORNARINA ($$)
A good inexpensive family-run choice, in Montréal's Little Italy. Tasty, basic pastas, seafood, and meat dishes, as well as thin crust pizzas cooked in a wood-fired brick oven.

➕ B4 ✉ 6825 boulevard Saint-Laurent ☎ 514/271-1741 🕐 Mon–Fri lunch, dinner; Sat, Sun dinner 🚇 Castenau, Jean-Talon ❓ Reservations needed weekends

HERMÈS ($)
It isn't elegant, but old-timers swear this Greek eatery in Park Extension serves the best marinated octopus, braised veal, roasted goat, and stuffed squid in the city.

➕ A5 ✉ 1014 rue Jean-Talon Ouest ☎ 514/272-3880 🕐 Daily 11AM–4PM 🚇 Acadie

LE JARDIN DE PANOS ($$)
The best of the Greek eateries in the rue Duluth area, with good versions of standard dishes such as calamari and moussaka.

➕ E5 ✉ 521 rue Duluth Est ☎ 514/521-4206 🕐 Daily lunch, dinner 🚇 Sherbrooke, Mont-Royal

LE LATINI ($$$)
Lavish Italian restaurant with a terrace for alfresco summer dining.

➕ F7 ✉ 1130 rue Jeanne-Mance ☎ 514/861-3166 🕐 Mon–Fri lunch, dinner; Sat dinner 🚇 Place-d'Armes, Place-des-Arts ❓ Reservations required

MILOS ($$$)
One of the most beautiful and priciest restaurants in the city. Exquisite Greek seafood.

➕ D5 ✉ 5357 avenue du Parc ☎ 514/272-3522 🕐 Mon–Fri lunch, dinner; Sat, Sun dinner ❓ Reservations required; cab advised

IL MULINO ($$)
A family affair with wonderful antipasti—olive-rich focaccia bread, grilled hot peppers, stuffed eggplant, grilled portobello mushrooms with cheese.

➕ C4 ✉ 236 rue Saint-Zotique Est ☎ 514/273-5776 🕐 Tue–Sun lunch, dinner 🚇 Beaubien ❓ Reservations essential

PSAROTAVERNA DU SYMPOSIUM ($$)
Fish nets and marine colours, plus grilled fresh fish, shrimp, and octopus.

➕ E5 ✉ 3829 rue Saint-Denis ☎ 514/842-0867 🕐 Mon–Fri lunch, dinner; Sat, Sun dinner 🚇 Sherbrooke

TRE MARIE ($)
Hearty Italian fare is the trademark of this modest but popular restaurant.

➕ B4 ✉ 6934 rue Clark ☎ 514/842-0867 🕐 Daily dinner 🚇 De Castelnau ❓ Reservations essential

HABITANT FOOD

One of the hardest things to find in Montréal is the hearty Québécois food the French pioneers developed to help them survive harsh winters and hard-working summers—thick pea soup, spicy *tourtière* (a kind of meat pie), pigs' feet, game pie, meatball stew, and heavy, syrup-soaked desserts like sugar pie and *pudding au chomeur* (literally "unemployed pudding"). Two unpretentious places that offer these delicacies are the Binerie Mont Royal (✉ 367 avenue Mont-Royal Est ☎ 514/285-9078); and Chez Clo (✉ 3199 rue Ontario Est ☎ 514/522-5348).

Pan-Asian

POPULAR MESS

Québec's very own contribution to fast-food culture is something called poutine (literally "mess"). It consists of a huge plate of French fries, covered liberally with lumps of pale yellow cheeze curds and drowned in a gelatinous mass of thick, brown gravy. Some restaurants offer a "Michigan" or "Italian" version by replacing the gravy with meat sauce, and some very smart restaurants (notably Globe ► 66) do a haute-cuisine version. Another fast-food favourite is barbecued chicken, a crispy skin, spit-roasted bird served with a spicy sauce. The man who dreamed up the concept and helped design the first rotisserie is Swiss-born Marcel Mauron, who opened the Chalet Bar-B-Q in 1944. The Chalet's chicken is still the best (✚ C10 ✉ 5456 rue Sherbrooke Ouest ☎ 514/489-7235). The ubiquitous Saint-Hubert chain (named for the street where it started) also offers a presentable version (✚ E5 ✉ 4462 rue Saint-Denis ☎ 514/844-9521).

BON BLÉ RIZ ($$)

Lamb in a peppery anise-flavoured sauce and spicy shrimp are among the flamboyant dishes at this unpretentious restaurant.
✚ F6 ✉ 1437 boulevard Saint-Laurent ☎ 514/844-1447
🕐 Mon–Fri lunch, dinner; Sat dinner 🚇 Saint-Laurent

CHAO PHRAYA ($)

A longtime Thai favourite, with over 100 dishes.
✚ D5 ✉ 50 boulevard Laurier Ouest at rue Saint-Urbain
☎ 514/272-5339
🕐 Sat–Wed dinner; Thu, Fri lunch, dinner 🚌 29

CHU CHAI ($$)

This vegetarian paradise whips up fine renditions of Thai classic dishes with substituted soy or seitan for chicken and shrimp.
✚ D5 ✉ 4088 rue Saint-Denis
☎ 514/843-4194 🕐 Daily lunch, dinner 🚇 Sherbrooke, Mont-Royal

ESCALÉ A SÀIGON ($$)

The French ruled Saigon for decades, and it shows in the Escale's anise-flavoured sliced eel and the crêpes stuffed with steamed rice.
✚ D5 ✉ 107 avenue Laurier Ouest ☎ 514/272-3456
🕐 Daily lunch, dinner
🚇 Laurier

MIKADO ($$)

The sushi's good and the excellent cooked food includes such delicacies as soft-shelled crabs in ginger, and grilled eel.
✚ D5 ✉ 368 avenue Laurier Ouest ☎ 514/279-4809
🕐 Mon– Fri lunch, dinner; Sat, Sun dinner 🚇 Laurier 🚌 51

MONGOLIE GRILL ($)

Select your meat (marinated), seafood, and vegetables from the buffet before it's flash cooked. Pay by the gram. Soup and appetizers are included. Discount for vegetarians.
✚ G6 ✉ 1180 rue Wolfe
☎ 514/526-0605 🕐 Mon–Fri lunch, dinner; Sat, Sun dinner
🚇 Beaudry ❓ Reservations recommended

NAGOYA ($$)

This is an ideal place to stop on a tour of Vieux-Montréal. Grilled, spicy beef, salmon, chicken, and squid are served in lacquered boxes along with salad, sticky rice, and Korean condiments.
✚ G7 ✉ 140 rue Notre-Dame Ouest ☎ 514/845-5864
🕐 Mon–Sun 11AM–10PM
🚇 Place d'Armes
❓ Reservations recommended

ORCHIDÉEDE CHINE ($$$)

Best of the Tuxedo Chinese restaurants: flash-fried spinach and dumpling with peanut sauce served in an elegantly simple setting.
✚ E7 ✉ 2017 rue Peel
☎ 514/287-1878 🕐 Mon–Fri lunch, dinner; Sat dinner
🚇 Peel

SOUVENIRS DE BANGKOK ($$)

The seafood dishes here are the best—sautéed squid with crunchy spinach and peanuts. Vegetarian menu.
✚ E8 ✉ 1925 rue Sainte-Catherine Ouest
☎ 514/938-2235 🕐 Mon–Fri lunch, dinner; Sat dinner
🚇 Guy-Concordia

Other Ethnic Cuisines

L'ACTUEL ($$)

This noisy downtown café is known for its Belgian dishes, offering several variations on the theme of mussels and French fries.

✚ F8 ✉ 1194 rue Peel ☎ 514/866-1537 🕐 Mon–Fri lunch, dinner; Sat dinner 🚇 Peel, Bonaventure

BYBLOS ($)

Books and Scrabble games provide a backdrop for such Iranian dishes as spinach yoghurt and chicken koukou.

✚ E4 ✉ 1499 avenue Laurier Est ☎ 514/523-9396 🕐 Tue–Sun lunch, dinner 🚇 Laurier 🚌 27

DELICES DE L'ÎLE MAURICE ($)

This tiny, colourful restaurant brings the flavours of Mauritius to suburban Verdun with its blend of Arab-French-English-Indian-African-Chinese influences.

✚ F11 ✉ 272 avenue Hickson ☎ 514/768-6023 🕐 Mon–Fri lunch, dinner; Sat dinner 🚇 Laurier 🚌 27

CAFÉ FERRARI ($$$)

Haute cuisine Portuguese style. Nibble on salted cod and olives while you consider the grilled octopus or the sausages marinated in red wine.

✚ E7 ✉ 1446 rue Peel ☎ 514/848-0988 🕐 Mon–Fri lunch, dinner; Sat dinner 🚇 Peel ❓ Reservations essential

GOLDEN CURRY ($)

This crowded, hole in the wall in the north-end Laurier district has some of the best Indian food in Montréal. The tandoori dishes are especially good and the $5 lunch is a steal.

✚ D5 ✉ 5210 boulevard Saint-Laurent ☎ 514/270-2561 🕐 Daily lunch, dinner 🚇 Laurier 🚌 51

JANO ($$)

This Portuguese grill produces delectable lamb chops, sardines, trout, and sausages dabbed with a little pepper oil.

✚ F6 ✉ 3883 boulevard Saint-Laurent ☎ 514/849-0646 🕐 Thu–Sat lunch, dinner; Sun, Mon dinner 🚇 Saint-Laurent 🚌 55

PUCAPUCA ($)

Rabbit with roasted peanuts and quail in mango sauce highlight owner Ciro Wong's Peruvian menu.

✚ D5 ✉ 5400 boulevard Saint-Laurent ☎ 514/272-8029 🕐 Tue–Sat lunch, dinner 🚇 Laurier

SENZALA ($$)

This restaurant is known for its Brazilian-style dishes such as squid in garlic and *mariscada* (fish, clams, and pork in a white-wine sauce).

✚ C5 ✉ 177 avenue Bernard Ouest ☎ 514/274-1464 🕐 Mon–Fri lunch, dinner; Sat, Sun brunch, dinner 🚌 55

CAFÉ STASH ($$)

Here you sit on pews to consume Polish dishes—hot borscht, pierogi, and several kinds of sausage.

✚ G7 ✉ 200 rue Saint-Paul Ouest ☎ 514/845-6611 🕐 Daily lunch, dinner 🚇 Place d'Armes

CHEAP EATS

The best food court in town is upstairs in Le Faubourg Sainte-Catherine (✉ 1616 rue Sainte-Catherine Ouest). It has plenty of table space and is mercifully short on the usual chain operations, featuring instead a multifarious array of independents selling Moroccan, Italian, Szechuan, Lebanese, and Mexican dishes. The food courts in the Gare Centrale, Complexe Desjardins and Place Ville-Marie are a cut above the usual with stalls selling pastries, Mexican food, grilled sausages, smoked meat as well as the usual offerings of chicken, burgers, and fries. Little shops selling huge bowls of Vietnamese noodle soups have sprung up all over town, especially at the lower end of boulevard Saint-Laurent. They're good value, filling, and tasty.

Steaks & Deli Food

SMOKED MEAT AND BAGELS

Jewish refugees from eastern Europe—primarily Romania—started arrivng in the city in great numbers in the early decades of the 20th century. Like all other immigrants, they brought their traditional dishes. Two such delicacies that have become an integral part of Montréal diet are bagels (a very crusty version, baked in a wood-burning oven) and smoked meat, (served thin-sliced and heaped in rye-bread sandwiches). The meat is beef brisket that has been dry-cured in spices for several weeks and then smoked for a few hours. Former Montréalers of all ethnic backgrounds usually stock up on both these foods on visits home. For smoked meat they usually go to Schwartz's (see main entry this page), and for bagels it's either the Saint-Viateur Bagel Shop (✉ 263 rue Saint-Viateur ☎ 514/276-8044) or Fairmount Bagel Factory (✉ 74 rue Fairmount Ouest ☎ 514/272-0667).

BENS ($)
Opened in 1908 by Ben Kravitz and still run by his grandsons, this garishly lit barn is popular with clubbers and late moviegoers.
✚ E7 ✉ 990 boulevard de Maisonneuve ☎ 514/844-1000 ⏲ Daily breakfast, lunch, dinner. Until 5AM ☒ Peel

ENTRECÔTE SAINT-JEAN ($)
Bistro decor with a simple and inexpensive menu—walnut salad, sirloin, perfect crunchy fries, and chocolate profiteroles.
✚ F7 ✉ 2022 rue Peel ☎ 514/281-6492 ⏲ Mon–Fri lunch, dinner; Sat, Sun dinner ☒ Peel

MR. STEER ($)
A simple steakhouse with leatherette booths serving great burgers.
✚ E8 ✉ 1198 rue Saint-Catherine Ouest ☎ 514/866-3233 ⏲ Daily lunch, dinner ☒ Peel

MAGNAN ($$)
This popular tavern serves roast beef, steaks, and salmon pie to longshoremen, truckers, lawyers, and executives. On the Lachine Canal bicycle path.
✚ F9 ✉ 2602 rue Saint-Patrick ☎ 514/935-9647 ⏲ Daily lunch, dinner ☒ Charlevoix

THE MAIN ($)
Good neighbourhood deli with excellent smoked meat.
✚ E5 ✉ 3864 boulevard Saint-Laurent ☎ 514/843-8126 ⏲ Daily breakfast, lunch, dinner ☒ Mont-Royal

MOISHE'S ($$$)
Marbled steaks aged the same way since 1938. Crowded and noisy.
✚ E6 ✉ 3961 boulevard Saint-Laurent at rue Duluth ☎ 514/845-3509 ⏲ Daily dinner ☒ Mont-Royal

LA PARYSE ($)
The burgers at this Quartier-Latin spot are huge and the fries are excellent. Toppings for designer hamburgers include blue cheese, cream cheese, porcino mushrooms, and fresh-grated Parmesan. Very popular with students at the nearby junior college.
✚ F6 ✉ 302 rue Ontario Est ☎ 514/842-2040 ⏲ Daily lunch, dinner ☒ Berri-UQAM

QUEUE DE CHEVAL ($$$)
Classy steakhouses with prices to match. Well-aged, thick, marbled slabs of beef are sold by weight and seared at an open grill with a copper chimney. Conspicuous consumption will result in a tight belt and a thin wallet.
✚ F8 ✉ 1221 boulevard René-Lévesque Ouest ☎ 514/390-0090 ⏲ Daily lunch, dinner ☒ Lucien-L'Allier

SCHWARTZ'S ($)
The three best things on the menu are smoked meat, smoked meat, and smoked meat—but the steaks are pretty good too. Famous and packed, expect brusque service and queues.
✚ E5 ✉ 3895 boulevard Saint-Laurent at rue Napoléon ☎ 514/842-4813 ⏲ Daily lunch, dinner ☒ Mont-Royal

Cafés & Pâtisseries

AMBIANCE ($)

This quirky on Antique Row serves salads, sandwiches, and imaginatively sauced pastas. Busy at lunch.

✚ F8 ✉ 1874 rue Notre-Dame Ouest ☎ 514/939-2609 🕓 Wed–Sat 11–5; Sun–Tue 11–4.40PM. Jan, Feb: closed Sat. Dinner by arrangement only Ⓜ Lucien-l'Allier

L'ANECDOTE ($)

This neighbourhood spot, hung with movie posters and old Coke ads, does a great line in vegetarian sandwiches.

✚ E5 ✉ 801 rue Rachel Est, near rue Saint-Hubert ☎ 514/526-7967 🕓 Daily breakfast, lunch, dinner Ⓜ Mont-Royal

LA BRIOCHE LYONNAISE ($)

The best pâtisserie in a city known for its cakes and confectioners. The chocolates are sensational.

✚ F6 ✉ 1593 rue Saint-Denis between boulevard de Maisonnneuve and rue Emery ☎ 514/842-7017 🕓 Daily breakfast, lunch, dinner Ⓜ Berri-UQAM

CLAUDE POSTEL ($)

Opened by former employees of Montréal's great restaurateur, Claude Postel, this chic café in Vieux-Montréal makes chocolates, pastries, and first-class sandwiches, as well as hot lunches. In summer it produces decadently rich gelatto-like ice cream.

✚ G7 ✉ 75 rue Notre-Dame Ouest ☎ 514/844-8750 🕓 Daily lunch Ⓜ Place d'Armes

LES GÂTERIES CAFÉ ($)

Haunt of writers and artists. The house coffee is a rich blend of 40 kinds of beans.

✚ F6 ✉ 3443 rue Saint-Denis ☎ 514/843-6235 🕓 Daily breakfast, lunch, dinner Ⓜ Sherbrooke

CAFÉ GRANO ($)

Deliberately seedy and singularly ungracious, but the sandwiches—combos like smoked chicken, bocconcini, pesto, and tomatoes—are superb.

✚ F6 ✉ 3597 boulevard Saint-Laurent ☎ 514/840-9000 🕓 Daily from 11.30 Ⓜ Saint-Laurent 🚌 51

PÂTISSERIE BELGE ($)

This cheerful café/tearoom is an ideal place to stop after a stroll on Mont Royal for a café au lait and a rich Belgian chocolate confection. The soups, salads, and pâtés are all good.

✚ E6 ✉ 3485 avenue du Parc ☎ 514/845-1245 🕓 Closes: Mon–Wed 6PM; Thu–Fri 8PM; Sat 5.30PM; Sun 4.30PM Ⓜ Place-des-Arts métro and then 10-minute walk

CAFÉ SANTROPOL ($)

A charming student and alternative café with largely vegetarian food, and over 60 herbal teas on offer. Many ice creams, malts, and sodas, and plenty of fruit juices, salads, and quiches.

✚ E6 ✉ 3990 rue Saint-Urbain ☎ 514/842-3110 🕓 Tue–Fri lunch, dinner; Sat dinner; Sun brunch, dinner Ⓜ Sherbrooke

OPEN-AIR CAFÉS

Good coffee and reasonably priced snacks are available in just about any open-air café. Find a busy one, pick a sunny table, and sit for as long as you want watching the world go by. The 50 or so cafés in the A. L. Van Houtte chain, a company that started life as a coffee importer in 1919, are very reliable. Other good locally owned chains are the Brulerie Saint-Denis and the Café Depôt. The Toronto-based Second Cup is making serious inroads, sprouting up all over the place and the US giant Starbuck's, has started to proliferate.

Art & Antiques

WHERE TO LOOK

Antique hunters with thick wallets search for treasures in the lavish shops along rue Sherbrooke Ouest and in exclusive Westmount. The more modest crowd look on trendy Antique Alley on rue Notre-Dame Ouest. Real hunters haunt the shops on rue Amherst, where they can buy wooden toys in Antiquités Curiosités at No. 1769, or scavenge chrome fittings from the 1950s in Cité Déco at No. 1761.

L'ANTIQUAIRE JOYAL

Religious art and other relics of early Québec, plus Victorian furniture.

✚ G5 ✉ 1475 rue Amherst
☎ 514/524-0057
🚇 Beaudry

ANTIQUITÉS PHYLLIS FRIEDMAN

Excellent English and European furniture and decorative accessories—Anglo-Irish glass, Oriental porcelain, and crystal.

✚ E8 ✉ 1776 rue Sherbrooke Ouest ☎ 514/935-1991
🕐 Mon–Fri 10.30–6; Sat 10.30–5 🚇 Guy Métro

LE CHARIOT

The country's largest gallery devoted to Inuit art, one of the most distinctive and purely Canadian of souvenirs.

✚ G7 ✉ 446 place Jacques-Cartier ☎ 514/875-4994
🚌 38 🚇 Champ-de-Mars

COACH HOUSE ANTIQUES

China, silverware, fine art, jewellery, and furniture.

✚ D9 ✉ 135 avenue Greene
☎ 514/937-6191 🕐 Mon–Fri 10–6; Sat 10–5 🚇 Atwater

GUILDE CANADIENNE DES MÉTIERS D'ART

Canadian crafts such as blown glass, porcelain, pewter, tapestry, and jewellery, plus a permanent exhibition of Inuit, First Peoples, and other Canadian sculpture, prints, and artefacts.

✚ E7 ✉ 1460 rue Sherbrooke Ouest ☎ 514/849-6091; www.canadianguild.com
🕐 Mon–Fri 10–6; Sat 10–5
🚇 Guy-Concordia

HENRIETTA ANTONY

Large shop spread over four floors, which majors in fine chandeliers and lamps.

✚ D9 ✉ 4192 rue Sainte-Catherine Ouest at avenue Greene ☎ 514/935-9116 🕐 Tue–Fri 10–5.30; Sat 10–3 🚇 Atwater

LE VILLAGE DES ANTIQUAIRES

Fourteen dealers share this shop, among them specialists in furniture, jewellery, books, and vintage clothing.

✚ E9 ✉ 1708 rue Notre-Dame Ouest ☎ 514/931-5121
🕐 Daily 11–5
🚇 Lionel-Groulx

LUCIE FAVREAU SPORTS MEMORABILIA

Just the place to pick up a hockey stick autographed by a 1950s great or a 1940s soccer poster.

✚ E9 ✉ 1904 rue Notre-Dame Ouest ☎ 514/989-5117
🕐 Mon–Sat 12–5
🚇 Lionel-Groulx

PARENT MOQUIN ANTIQUITÉS

Lots of small sterling, silver plate, and fine china.

✚ F9 ✉ 1650 rue Notre-Dame Ouest near rue Richmond ☎ 514/933-9435 🕐 Mon–Fri 11–6; Sat 11–5; Sun 12–5
🚇 Lucien l'Allier

PETIT MUSÉE

Sensational antiques from around the world, at stratospheric prices. Worth a visit even if you don't intend to buy.

✚ E8 ✉ 1494 rue Sherbrooke Ouest ☎ 514/937-6161
🕐 Tue–Sat 10–5
🚇 Guy-Concordia

Books & Newspapers

BIBLIOMANIA BOOK SHOPPE
One of the city's best second-hand shops with titles in French and English.
D6 ✉ 1841 rue Sainte-Catherine Ouest ☎ 514/933-8156 🕐 Mon–Fri 11.30–6.30; Sat 11–6; Sun 12.30–2 🚇 Guy-Concordia 🚌 15

DOUBLE HOOK CANADIAN BOOKS
Canadian literature and children's books in a charming Victorian house in Westmount.
D9 ✉ 1235 avenue Greene at rue Sainte-Catherine Ouest ☎ 514/932-5093 🕐 Mon–Wed 9.30–5.30; Thu, Fri 9.30–8; Sat 9.30–5 🚇 Atwater

EX LIBRIS
This elegant building on rue Sherbrooke houses a fine collection of second-hand books.
E8 ✉ 1628b rue Sherbrooke Ouest ☎ 514/932-1689 🕐 Mon–Thu 11–6; Fri 11–8; Sat 11–5 🚇 Guy-Concordia

INDIGO
This bright, airy branch of a Toronto-based chain, in Place Montréal Trust, has a café and a huge selection of books.
F7 ✉ 1500 avenue McGill ☎ 514/281-5549 🕐 Daily 9AM–11PM 🚇 McGill

LIBRAIRIE RENAUD-BRAY
Predominantly French-language chain for books, CDs, magazines, and stationery.
B8 ✉ 5225 Côtes-des-Neiges ☎ 514/342-1515 🕐 Daily 8AM–midnight 🚇 Côte-des-Neiges

NICHOLAS HOARE BOOKS
Best for British titles, "beaux-livres," and classical and jazz CDs.
D9 ✉ 1366 avenue Greene ☎ 514/933-4201 🕐 Mon–Wed 9.30–6; Thu, Fri 9.30–9; Sat 9–5; Sun 12–5 🚇 Atwater

PARAGRAPHE BOOK STORE
Popular with serious book lovers and students. Lectures and readings by leading Canadian authors.
E7 ✉ 2220 avenue McGill College ☎ 514/845-5811 🕐 Mon–Fri 7AM–11PM; Sat, Sun 9AM–11PM 🚇 McGilll

ULYSSES LA LIBRAIRIE DU VOYAGE
Travel books in French and English, as well as maps and assorted travel-related artefacts. Several locations.
F7 ✉ 560 avenue du Président-Kennedy near avenue Union ☎ 514/843-7222 🕐 Mon–Wed 10–6; Thu, Fri 10–8; Sat 10–5; Sun 12–5 🚇 McGill

UNIVERSITÉ MCGILL
Well-stocked and intelligent book shelves.
E7 ✉ 3420 rue McTavish ☎ 514/398-7444 🕐 Mon–Sat 8.30AM–10PM 🚇 Peel

THE WORD
An eccentric shop with books on philosophy, art, and literature. Cash only.
E7 ✉ 469 rue Milton ☎ 514/845-5640 🕐 Mon–Wed 10–6; Thu–Fri 10–9; Sat 11–6 🚇 McGill

GLOBAL PRESS
For foreign newspapers try:
Metropolitan News
✉ 1109 rue Cypress at the corner of Peel, near Square-Dorchester ☎ 514/866-9227
Multimags
✉ 1570 boulevard de Maisonneuve Ouest, near rue Mackay ☎ 514/935-7044
Maison de la Presse Internationale
✉ 728 rue Sainte-Catherine Ouest ☎ 514/954-0333

Men's & Women's Clothes

RUE CHABANEL

The heart and soul of Canada's garment industry is compressed into an eight-block stretch of this street in Montréal's "north" end. And every Saturday from about 8.30 to 1, the area's dozens of tiny factories and importers open to the public. Bargains abound and prices often "include taxes" if you pay cash. Start at boulevard Saint-Laurent and work your way "west."

TAXES

Federal and provincial taxes on most purchases total a little over 15 percent. You can reclaim this on purchases of $100 and over (▶ 90).

ANGELINA LEATHER

Stylish leather clothes at reasonable prices for men and women.
✚ F7 ✉ 625 rue Sainte-Catherine Ouest ☎ 514/987-1459 ⏰ Mon–Fri 10–6; Sat 10–5; Sun 12–5 Ⓜ McGill

LA CACHE

The premier store of a chain covering Canada selling pretty store-label clothes, linens, and gifts.
✚ D9 ✉ 1353 avenue Greene near rue Sherbrooke Ouest ☎ 514/935-4361 ⏰ Mon–Wed 9.30–6; Thu, Fri 9.30–7; Sat 9.30–5; Sun 12–5 Ⓜ Atwater

CHAS JOHNSON & SONS

This fine traditional tailor's shop with three kilt makers on call is one of the few places in Canada still offering made-to-measure Highland regalia. It also stocks the necessary Scottish accessories—hose, sporrans, jackets, skean-dhus—as well as a full line of men's wear.
✚ F7 ✉ 1184 place Philippe (near boulevard René-Lévesque) ☎ 514/878-1931 ⏰ Tue–Fri 9–5.30; Sat 9.30–4.30 Ⓜ McGill

DUBUC MODE DE VIE

Philippe Dubuc is one of the premier designers of both men's and women's clothes in Canada. This stylish boutique in the Plateau Mont-Royal district is his headquarters and displays both collections in gorgeous surroundings.
✚ E5 ✉ 4451 rue Saint-Denis ☎ 514/282-1424; www.dubucmodedevie.com ⏰ Mon–Wed 10.30–6; Thu, Fri 10.30–9; Sat 10.30–5; Sun 1–5 Ⓜ Mont-Royal

GIORGIO

Two chic stores offer top names in men's and women's high fashion.
✚ E7 ✉ Giorgio Femme (women): Le Cours Mont-Royal, 1455 rue Peel ☎ 514/282-0294 ✉ Giorgio Montréal (men): Maison Ican 1176 rue Sherbrooke Ouest ☎ 514/287-1928 ⏰ Mon–Wed 9.30–6; Thu, Fri 9.30–9; Sat 9.30–5.30 Ⓜ Peel

NADYA TOTO

Nadya Toto designs modern, elegantly casual but reasonably priced clothes for women 25 to 55. This young designer often works with a wool-Spandex mix that gives her clothes comfort and softness.
✚ E7 ✉ 2057 rue de la Montagne ☎ 514/350-9090 ⏰ Mon–Wed 10–6; Thu, Fri 11–9; Sat 11–5; Sun 12–5 Ⓜ Peel

PIERRE, JEAN, JACQUES

Dressy and casual clothes for men, with an emphasis on Canadian design.
✚ D5 ✉ 150 avenue Laurier Ouest ☎ 514/270-8392 Ⓜ Laurier 🚌 51

SCARLETT O'HARA

Ultratrendy shop with its own line of daring women's fashions.
✚ E5 ✉ 254 avenue Mont-Royal Est ☎ 514/844-9435 ⏰ Mon–Wed 11–6; Thu, Fri 11–9; Sat 11–5 Ⓜ Mont-Royal

Accessories & Fine Jewellery

BIRKS

One of the country's most prestigious and longest-established jewellers, particularly known for its silverware and classy blue packaging. You'll also find high-quality china and crystal. Of the several city locations, this branch is particularly worth a visit just for a look at its wonderfully striking art deco interior.

🚇 F7 ✉ 1240 Square Phillips
☎ 514/397-2511
🕐 Mon–Wed 10–6; Thu, Fri 10–9; Sat 9.30–5; Sun 12–5
Ⓜ McGill

BROWN CHAUSSURES

Fashionable and expensive men's and women's shoes, boots, and bags. This popular chain has half a dozen outlets around the city.

🚇 F7 ✉ 1 place Ville-Marie, rue University
☎ 514/861-8925
🕐 Mon–Wed 10–5; Thu, Fri 10–9; Sat 9–5; Sun 12–5
Ⓜ McGill, Bonaventure

CHAPOFOLIE

Both men and women can complete their fashion purchases here, at the largest hat store in the city.

🚇 E5 ✉ 3944 rue Saint-Denis
☎ 514/982-0036 🕐 Tue–Thu 12–6; Fri 12–9; Sat, Sun 12–5
Ⓜ Mont-Royal

HEMSLEYS

Montréal's oldest jewellers; they also sell silverware and china.

🚇 F7 ✉ 660 rue Sainte-Catherine Ouest
☎ 514/866-3706
🕐 Mon–Wed 10–6; Thu, Fri 10–9; Sat 12–5 Ⓜ McGill

HENRI HENRI

Men with a sense of style have been buying their Borsalinos and Stetsons from this east-end haberdashery since 1932.

🚇 F6 ✉ 189 rue Sainte-Catherine Est
☎ 514/288-0109
🕐 Mon–Thu 9–6; Fri 9–9; Sat 9–5 Ⓜ Saint-Laurent

KAUFMANN DE SUISSE

Craftsmen here produce their own line of exclusive jewellery.

🚇 E8 ✉ 2195 rue Crescent
☎ 514/848-0595
🕐 Mon–Fri 9.30–5.30; Sat 10–5 Ⓜ Guy-Concordia

LILI-LES-BAINS

Designer Louise Daoustaï's tiny workshop/boutique in the rundown Saint-Henri district makes fine made-to-measure bathing suits for women of all sizes. The shop has branched out into making made-to-measure clothes too, from skirts to evening gowns. Telephone before you go.

🚇 F6 ✉ 1336 rue Notre-Dame Ouest ☎ 514/937-9197
🕐 Wed, Fri 10–6; Thu 10–8; Sat 9–2 Ⓜ Lucien l'Allier

SOXBOX ACCESSORIES

Come to this spot slightly south of downtown if you are desperate to find exactly the right socks, stockings, or tights. Top European and North American manufacturers are represented.

🚇 D9 ✉ 1357 avenue Greene at the corner of rue Sherbrooke Ouest ☎ 514/931-4980 🕐 Mon–Fri 9–6; Sat 9–5
Ⓜ Atwater

FURS

Montréal owes its early commercial success to the fur trades, and trends away from the wearing of furs notwithstanding, the city still boasts some of Canada's best furriers. Grosvenor-McComber (✉ 402 boulevard de Maisonneuve Ouest ☎ 514/288-1255) has been in business since 1895. Birger Christensen at Holt Renfrew (✉ 1300 rue Sherbrooke Ouest ☎ 514/842-5111) is a favourite among the city elite.

Gifts

SWEET AND MUSICAL

Looking for something "typical" to take home? For something sweet, think maple. Québec produces more than two-thirds of the world's supply of maple syrup so, not surprisingly, the stuff is ubiquitous on Montréal breakfast tables, and confectionery, butter, and sugar made from maple sap are common treats. The best time to buy is in spring when the supply is plentiful. Best prices are at farmers' markets (► 77).

For something tonier, consider music. Because of its linguistic isolation, Québec has produced a rich popular culture of its own that's better known in France than in the US or even the rest of Canada. Try Archambault (see main entry this page) for the latest hits, or look for recordings by chansonniers Gilles Vigneault and Félix Leclerc or seminal rock musician Robert Charlebois.

ARCHAMBAULT

Montréal's own music shop is excellent for current releases, classical music, and Québec pop. It also has an extensive selection of song books and sheet music.

➕ F5 ✉ 175 rue Sainte-Catherine Est
☎ 514/281-0367
🕐 Mon–Wed 9.30–7; Thu, Fri 9.30–9; Sat, Sun 11–5
Ⓜ Berri-UQAM

CANADIENS BOUTIQUE

Posters, pucks, jerseys, and other memorabilia, all bearing the storied team emblem.

➕ F8 ✉ Molson Centre, 1260 rue de la Gauchetière
☎ 514/989-2836
🕐 Mon–Wed 9.30–6; Thu, Fri 9.30–9; Sat 9.30–5
Ⓜ Bonaventure

DAVIDOFF TABAC

Top-quality cigars from around the world, as well as pipes, hardwood cigar boxes, and other smoking paraphernalia.

➕ E7 ✉ 1458 rue Sherbrooke Ouest ☎ 514/289-9118
🕐 Mon–Wed 10–6; Thu, Fri 10–9; Sat 10–6; Sun 11–4
Ⓜ Guy

EDIFICE BELAGO

This building is essentially a mall for art galleries, showing established and upcoming artists. Some of the best include Troise Pointes and Optica Centre for Contemporary Art .

➕ F7 ✉ 372 rue Sainte-Catherine Ouest ☎ Troise Pointes 514/866-8008; Optica 514/874-1666
🕐 Wed–Fri 12–6; Sat 12–5
Ⓜ Place-des-Arts

HMV

Airy, comprehensive, and well organized—the best place to buy CDs and audiocassettes.

➕ F7 ✉ 1020 rue Sainte-Catherine Ouest ☎ 514/875-0765 🕐 Mon–Fri 9.30–9; Sat 9–5; Sun 10–5 Ⓜ Peel

KANUK

Here you can find everything you need to survive when the temperature drops.

➕ E5 ✉ 485 rue Rachel Est
☎ 514/284-4494
🕐 Mon–Wed 9–6; Thu, Fri 9–9; Sat 9.30–5; Sun 11–5 Ⓜ Mont-Royal 🚌 30

LINEN CHEST

Simply the best for bedding, towels, kitchen linen, and the like.

➕ F7 ✉ Promenades de la Cathédrale, 625 rue Sainte-Catherine Ouest ☎ 514/282-9525 🕐 Mon–Wed 10–6; Thu, Fri 10–9; Sat 10–5; Sun 12–5 Ⓜ McGill

LA MAISON DU STYLO PEEL

Lovely pens and pencils.

➕ F7 ✉ 1212 avenue Union
☎ 514/866-1340 🕐 Mon–Fri 8–5.30; Sat 10–4 Ⓜ McGill

OINKOINK

Toys and fashion for young children.

➕ D10 ✉ 1343 avenue Greene ☎ 514/939-2634
🕐 Mon–Fri 9.30–6; Sat 9.30–5; Sun 11–9 Ⓜ Atwater

WORN DOORSTEP

Finest collection of quality Canadian souveniers.

➕ G6 ✉ 350 rue Saint-Paul Marché Bonsecours ☎ 514/397-0666 🕐 Sat–Wed 10–6; Thu–Fri 10–9 Ⓜ Champ-de-Mars

Markets

LE FAUBOURG SAINTE-CATHERINE

The Faubourg complex is easily accessible from downtown. Clothing and craft outlets compete with food, fruit, and vegetable stalls over three levels while inexpensive cafés and food kiosks surround a central atrium.

☩ E7 ✉ Rue Guy at rue Sainte-Catherine Ouest
☎ 514/939-3663 🕐 Daily 9AM–9.30PM 🚇 Guy-Concordia

MARCHÉ ATWATER

This market is known for meat and vegetables. It is close to a Métro station and near the Lachine Canal towpath. It's also a great place to buy delicious maple syrup.

☩ E10 ✉ 138 avenue Atwater
☎ 514/937-7754
🕐 Mon–Wed 8–6; Thu–Fri 8AM–9PM; Sat 8–6; Sun 8–5
🚇 Lionel-Groulx

MARCHÉ ST-JACQUES

Within walking distance of the Quartier Latin and devoted to plants and flowers, this market is pretty enough to visit for its own sake.

☩ F5 ✉ Rue Ontario Est at rue Amherst ☎ 514/937-7754
🕐 May–Oct: Mon–Wed 7–6; Thu, Fri 7AM–9PM; Sat, Sun 7–5
🚇 Sherbrooke, Beaudry

MARCHÉ JEAN-TALON

Montréal's largest public market lies some distance from downtown, but is just a 5 minute walk from two Métro stations and lies at the heart of Montréal's Little Italy.

☩ B3–B4 ✉ Rue Jean-Talon Est between avenues Henri-Julien and Casgrain
☎ 514/277-1588
🕐 Mon–Wed 8–6; Thu, Fri 8AM–9PM; Sat 8–6; Sun 8–5
🚇 Jean-Talon, De Castelnau

MARCHÉ LACHINE

The location of this small farmers' market near the end of the lovely Lachine Canal towpath makes it a delightful place to stop for picnic fixings.

☩ Off map at A13 ✉ Corner of 17ième avenue and rue Piché in Lachine 🕐 Mon–Wed 7–6; Thu, Fri 7AM–9PM; Sat 7–5

MARCHÉ DE L'OUEST

One of the island's most popular markets is deep in the West Island suburbs. Look for quality butchers, fishmongers, bulk spice shops, bakeries, and patisseries. From early summer to late autumn, farmers sell flowers, berries, vegetables, honey, and maple products outdoors too.

☩ Off map at A13 ✉ 11,600 de Salaberry, Dollard-des-Armeaux ☎ 514/685-0119
🕐 Sat–Wed 9–6; Thu, Fri 9–9

MARCHÉ MAISONNEUVE

The original Marché Maisonneuve, a magnificent Beaux Arts building dating from 1912, is now a cultural centre, but farmers continue to sell their produce in this more modern building right next door. Flowers, pastries, local wine and cheese, and other traiditonal products can all be bought here.

☩ H1–H2 ✉ 4445 rue Ontario Est ☎ 514/937-7754
🕐 Mon–Wed, Sat 8–6; Thu–Fri 8–9; Sun 8–5 🚇 Pie-XI

FLEAS MOVE OUT

The Vieux-Port closed the only flea market of any size within Montréal's city limits several years ago to make way for the city's science centre. But there are several good-size markets on the city perimeter. The best by far is Finnegans (☩ off map at A13 ✉ 700 Main Road, Hudson ☎ 450/458-4377 🕐 May–Oct: Sat), which has been operating for 26 years in a barn and an adjoining field on the outskirts of town in the semi-rural hamlet of Hudson. While not the region's biggest market, its merchandise is several notches above the norm. At least 100 merchants and dealers sell clocks, silverware, dishes, glassware, wood-carvings of herons and roosters, wrought-iron goods, plants, furniture, dried flowers, honey, lampshades, jewellery, and period collectables. Many Montréalers make a day out of an excursion, stopping for lunch or dinner at the Willow Inn (✉ 208 Maid Road ☎ 450/458-7006).

Malls & Department Stores

MALL SHOPPING

The great advantage of shopping in Montreal's state-of-the-art malls, of course, is that it's an all-season endeavour–an important consideration in a city with cruel winters and hot, humid summers. Most of them are linked into the Underground City's (► 36) extensive network of tunnels and Métro lines. Many of the city's major department stores are also connected to the system, and some of them–notably fashionable competitors Ogilvy (► 79) and Holt Renfrew (see entry this page)–have become mini-malls, opening shops within shops to showcase such designers as Jean-Claude Chacok, Guy Laroche, Lily Simon, and Cacherel.

LE CENTRE EATON

Ironically, the venerable Canadian department store that gave this mall its name closed its doors in 1999. But the mall—the largest in the downtown core with five floors of boutiques and shops—is still thriving.
➕ F7 ✉ 705 rue Sainte-Catherine Ouest ☎ 514/288-3708 ⏰ Mon—Fri 10–9; Sat 10–5; Sun 12–5 🚇 McGill

COMPLEXE DESJARDINS

This vast multitiered complex, one of the largest malls in eastern downtown, belongs to the powerful Mouvement Desjardins conglomerate. In addition to about 100 shops you'll find restaurants and bistros, walk-in dental and medical facilities, cinemas, offices, and a large piazza used for cultural events. Fountains and exotic plants make the place unusually pleasurable.
➕ F7 ✉ Rue Sainte-Catherine Ouest at Saint-Urbain ☎ 514/281-1870 ⏰ Mon—Wed 9.30–6; Thu, Fri 9.30–9; Sat 9.30–5; Sun 12–5 🚇 Place-des-Arts

LES COURS MONT-ROYAL

This elegant shopping centre is in the old Mount Royal Hotel, a jazz-age palace that was the largest hotel in the British Empire when it opened in 1922 with 1,100 rooms. When developers gutted the place in 1987, they left the exterior intact and saved part of the old lobby with a crystal chandelier that used to illuminate the Monte Carlo Casino. The inner court rises 10 stories to the roof, and is surrounded by balconies and fashionable shops.
➕ E7 ✉ 1550 rue Metcalfe 🚇 Peel

HOLT RENFREW

Established in 1837, this is the oldest of the city's large stores, and has occupied its present distinctive six-storey home since 1936. It is particularly known for its furs, and has supplied four generations of British royalty (among others), but also sells other quality goods and fashions.
➕ E7 ✉ 1300 rue Sherbrooke Ouest at rue de la Montagne ☎ 514/842-5111 ⏰ Mon—Wed 10–6; Thu, Fri 10–9; Sat 10–6; Sun 11.30 🚇 Peel

LA BAIE (THE BAY)

Construction of the establishment now known as La Baie in 1890 proved the catalyst for most of the subsequent retail development on rue Sainte-Catherine, Montréal's main shopping street. La Baie, successor to the venerable Hudson's Bay Company, emphasizes not only clothes but also other good, mid-range items, the most famous being the trademark Hudson's Bay coats and blankets.
➕ F7 ✉ 585 rue Sainte-Catherine Ouest ☎ 514/281-4422 ⏰ Mon—Wed 9.30–7; Thu–Fri 9.30–9; Sat–Sun 10–5 🚇 McGill

MARCHÉ BONSECOURS

The Marché Bonsecours is one of the most graceful buildings in Vieux-Montréal. Boutiques showcase local fashion, repro-antiques, and Canadian crafts. Of particular interest are the toys and gizmos for home and office you'll find in the gallery of the Institut de Design Montréal.

➕ G6 ✉ Rue Saint-Paul Street Est ☎ 514/872-7730
🕐 Sat–Wed 10–6; Thu, Fri 10–9 🚇 Champ-de-Mars

OGILVY

A favourite among affluent Montréalers, Ogilvy has been in business since 1866. The emphasis here is on luxury goods. A kilted bagpiper recalls the establishment's Scottish roots, piping at noon and again at closing.

➕ E8 ✉ 1307 rue Sainte-Catherine Ouest at rue de la Montagne ☎ 514/842-7711
🕐 Mon–Wed 10–6; Thu, Fri 10–9; Sat 9–6 🚇 Peel

PLACE MONTRÉAL TRUST

In this eye-catching glass tower, well over 120 shops share five shopping levels. Admire the stunning 30m (98ft) atrium.

➕ F7 ✉ Rue Sainte-Catherine Ouest at avenue McGill College ☎ 514/843-8000
🕐 Mon–Wed 10–6; Thu, Fri 10–9; Sat 10–5; Sun 12–5 🚇 McGill, Peel

PLACE VILLE-MARIE

This once-gloomy shopping mall now provides a home for over 100 retail outlets, many of them boutiques of top designers.

➕ F7 ✉ 1 place Ville-Marie ☎ 514/861-9393
🕐 Mon–Sat 9–6 🚇 Bonaventure

PROMENADES DE LA CATHÉDRALE

A popular place to stroll, the breathtaking Promenades are directly beneath Christ Church Cathedral. Look for the Linen Chest (➤ 76).

➕ F7 ✉ 625 rue Sainte-Catherine Ouest at rue University ☎ 514/849-9925
🕐 Mon–Wed 10–6; Thu, Fri 10–9; Sat 9–5; Sun 12–5 🚇 McGill

SIMONS

This Québec City-based department store sells its own line of sleek clothing for men, women, and kids; sweaters and hats are particularly good. The store shares the building with a cineplex and there is a good food court in the basement.

➕ F7 ✉ 977 rue Sherbrooke Ouest ☎ 514/282-1840
🕐 Mon–Wed 10–6; Thu, Fri 10–9; Sat 9.30–5; Sun 12–5 🚇 Peel/McGill

WESTMOUNT SQUARE

This small collection of exclusive shops is in the fashionable suburb of Westmount, underneath Ludwig Mies van der Rohe's minimalist tower. The food court sells pastries, pâtés, cheeses, and cakes. Adjacent avenue Greene is home to other interesting shops.

➕ E10 ✉ Avenue Greene at rue Sainte-Catherine Ouest 🚇 Atwater

SHOPPING DISTRICTS

Montréal's best shopping is in the malls close to the McGill Métro station and along rue Sainte-Catherine. Cheaper shops abound in Vieux-Montréal, notably on rues Notre-Dame and Saint-Jacques between rue McGill and place Jacques-Cartier. More Bohemian stores can be found around boulevard Saint-Laurent (The Main). Bookshops, galleries, and antiques shops are in nearby rue Saint-Denis, while still other interesting options are springing up around avenue du Mont-Royal and rue Saint-Viateur.

Bars

THE NAME'S THE GAME

If a friendly local suggests a watering hole (or a restaurant) make sure you get the full name and, if possible, the address. Because of the way the French language works and because of the loose definitions Québécois use, a place called, let's say, Au Henri could be listed under Bar Au Henri, Bistro Au Henri, Café Au Henri, Club Au Henri, Restaurant Au Henri, Salon Au Henri, or maybe even Au Henry, which could keep your fingers walking through the phone book for a while.

AU CÉPAGE

Professionals and journalists keep the place lively with talk and debate all week. Good food too.

✚ G7 ✉ 212 rue Notre-Dame Ouest ☎ 514/845-5436
🕐 Daily noon–2AM 🚇 Place d'Armes

CAFÉ CENTRAL

Small, relaxed, and convenient to shopping. Occasional live jazz.

✚ F5 ✉ 4479 rue Saint-Denis ☎ 514/845-9010 🕐 Daily 2.30PM–3AM 🚇 Sherbrooke

CAFÉ SARAJEVO

This eccentric little hangout on the edge of Chinatown appeals to artists, students, and local literati. Music on weekends ranges from blues to cabaret, all spiced up with a little belly dancing. Limited menu of eastern European food.

✚ F7 ✉ 2080 rue Clark ☎ 514/284-5629
🕐 Sun–Thu 5PM–1AM; Fri, Sat 5PM–3AM 🚇 Saint-Laurent

LE CHEVAL BLANC

Unchanged for half a century, music combines with the buzz of arty and political talk. Communal tables and beer brewed on the premises.

✚ F6 ✉ 809 rue Ontario Est ☎ 514/522-0211 🕐 Daily 3PM–3AM 🚇 Berri-UQAM

PUB LE VIEUX DUBLIN

A much-loved Irish pub popular among ex-patriots and Montréalers alike. Live Celtic music nights.

✚ F7 ✉ 1219a rue University near rue Sainte-Catherine Ouest ☎ 514/861-4448 🕐 Daily 11AM–2AM 🚇 McGill

PUB SIR WINSTON CHURCHILL

English-style pub known as "Winnies" with a dance floor.

✚ E8 ✉ 1459 rue Crescent ☎ 514/288-3814 🕐 Daily 11.30AM–3AM 🚇 Peel, Guy-Concordia

LE SAINT-SULPICE

Fashionable Quartier Latin bar, with terraces.

✚ F6 ✉ 1680 rue Saint-Denis near rue Emery ☎ 514/844-9458 🕐 Daily 11.30AM–3AM 🚇 Berri-UQAM

SHED CAFÉ

See and be seen in an industrial setting.

✚ F6 ✉ 3515 boulevard Saint-Laurent ☎ 514/842-0220 🕐 Daily 11AM–3AM 🚇 Saint-Laurent

STOGIE'S CAFÉ AND CIGARS

In the middle of a fashionable section of downtown. Antismoking proselytism not welcome.

✚ E8 ✉ 2015 rue Crescent ☎ 514/848-0069 🕐 Daily 11AM–3AM 🚇 Guy-Concordia

LE SWIMMING

Loft-style space with lots of art, large pool tables, and a huge TV.

✚ E6 ✉ 3643 boulevard Saint-Laurent ☎ 514/282-POOL 🚇 Saint-Laurent

ZIGGY'S PUB

Advertises itself as the place "where nobody knows your name"; quite friendly in its brusque way.

✚ E8 ✉ 1470 rue Crescent ☎ 514/285-8855
🕐 Mon–Thu 4PM–3AM; Fri–Sun 3PM–3AM 🚇 Guy-Concordia

Clubs & Discos

ANGELS

A club with two floors:
downstairs you watch
sports on a large-screen
TV; upstairs is for
chatting and high-energy
dancing.

➕ F6 ✉ 3604 boulevard
Saint-Laurent at rue Prince-Arthur
☎ 514/282-9944
🕐 Tue–Sat 9.30PM–3AM
🚍 29, 55

LE BALATTOU

A welcoming (if hot and
crowded) dance club with
an African and tropical
motif.

➕ E5 ✉ 4372 boulevard
Saint-Laurent ☎ 514/845-
5447 🕐 Tue–Sun 9PM–3AM
🚍 29, 55

BAR MINUIT

House, pop, retro, and
salsa play all night in this
crowded spot on
fashionable Laurier.

➕ D5 ✉ 115 rue Laurier
Ouest ☎ 514/271-2110
🕐 Wed–Sun 9PM–3AM
🚇 Laurier

BELMONT

Quiet bar with plenty
of room to sit and talk.
A disco is to the rear.
Long queues on
weekends.

➕ E5 ✉ 4483 boulevard
Saint-Laurent ☎ 514/845-
8443 🕐 Daily 8PM–3AM
🚍 29, 55 🎵 Cover charge on
weekends

CACTUS

This Mexican restaurant
turns into a frantic salsa
and Latin club, Y Lo
Mismo, after dark.

➕ E5 ✉ 4461 rue Saint-Denis
☎ 514/849-0349
🕐 Restaurant daily 2PM–10PM.
Club 10PM–3AM 🚇 Sherbrooke

CLUB LOUNGE KARINA'S

One of the biggest and
slickest clubs on trendy
rue Crescent features an
eclectic mix of Latin, jazz,
R & B, and hip hop. Live
and recorded music.

➕ E8 ✉ 1455 rue Crescent
☎ 514/288-0616 🕐 Tue–Fri
5PM–3AM; Sat–Sun 9PM–3AM
🚇 Guy-Concordia

CLUB 737

On top of Place Ville-
Marie, this is possibly the
most elegant disco in
town—it certainly has the
best views.

➕ F7 ✉ 1 place Ville-Marie
☎ 514/397-0737
🕐 Restaurant Mon–Fri lunch,
dinner; Sat dinner. Club Thu–Sat,
Mon 10PM–3AM
🚇 Bonaventure, McGill

JINGXI CLUB

Hip 20s and 30s listen to
heart-thumping mix of
electronic and house music
spun by the in-house DJ.
Big dance floor.

➕ E5 ✉ 401 rue Rachel Est
☎ 514/985-5464 🕐 Daily
10PM–3AM 🚇 Mont-Royal

LE PASSEPORT

By day a curiosity shop, by
night a long-running club
with a bar, dance floor,
good music.

➕ E5 ✉ 4156 rue Saint-Denis
☎ 514/842-6063 🕐 Nightly
🚇 Sherbrooke

SALSATHÈQUE

Popular downtown Latin
club; live music in
addition to house DJs.

➕ E7–F7 ✉ 1220 rue Peel at
rue Sainte-Catherine Ouest
☎ 514/875-0016
🕐 Wed–Sat 10PM–3AM
🚇 Peel

WHERE TO GO?

Clubs and discos are notorious
for fading in and out of
fashion, or for closing down
altogether, so for the latest on
clubs check the free
magazines to be found at
tourist offices, record shops,
and cafés. The *Mirror*, the
Hour and the French *Voir* (all
free) contain extensive listings
of clubs and live music
venues, as does *The Montréal
Gazette*, the city's main
English-language newspaper.
Remember that bars almost
always provide excellent food
as well as drinks. Many also
have live music (► 84), and
quite a few blur the
distinction between "bar,"
"club," and "café."

Cinema & The Performing Arts

TICKETS AND INFO

Tickets for individual shows and performances can be obtained directly from the box office of the venue concerned, or phone the central Admission office for information ☎ 514/790-1245 or 800/361-4595 (in Canada) or 800/675-5440 (in the US). Tickets for some events can also be obtained from the main Infotouriste office in Square-Dorchester or the lobbies of major hotels. For further details of performances consult the tourist office, look for flyers about the individual concerts, or search through the entertainment listings of major newspapers. You can also phone Info Arts Bell for events information ☎ 514/790-2787.

CINEMA

AMC 22 CINEMAS Á LA FORUM

This entertainment centre has 22 cinemas showing foreign and independent films in addition to Hollywood blockbusters. ✚ E9 ✉ 2313 rue Sainte-Catherine Ouest ☎ 514/904-1247 🚇 Atwater

EX CENTRIS

Showcases the best independent films and digital new-media works. ✚ F6 ✉ 3536 boulevard Saint-Laurent ☎ 514/847-3536; www.ex-centris.com 🚇 Atwater

FAMOUS PLAYERS PARAMOUNT

Downtown centre with 15 theatres—two with IMAX screens—that show films in French and English. ✚ F7 ✉ 977 rue Sainte-Catherine Ouest ☎ 514/842-5825 🚇 McGill

NATIONAL FILM BOARD OF CANADA

Produces full-length features, animated films, and documentaries. Viewing booths and theatres. ✚ F6 ✉ 1564 rue Saint-Denis ☎ 514/496-6887 🚇 Berri-UQAM

CINÉ EXPRESS CAFÉ

Drop in for a drink, a bite to eat, and an old flick. ✚ E8 ✉ 1926 rue Sainte-Catherine Ouest ☎ 514/939-CINE 🚇 Guy-Concordia

CIRCUS

CIRQUE DU SOLEIL

This circus has come a long way since it opened in a blue-and-yellow striped tent on the Montréal waterfront in 1984. Its combination of dance, acrobatics, costumes, and drama has made it an international hit. In the summer of odd-numbered years, the circus sets up in the grounds of its head-quarters and training school in a northeastern Montréal neighbourhood. ☎ 800/361-4595

CHURCH MUSIC

You can hear recitals and concerts of chamber, choral, and organ music in: **Basilique Notre-Dame** (▶ 40); **Christ Church Cathedral** (▶ 35); **Oratoire Saint-Joseph** (▶ 30); and **St. James United Church** ✚ F7 ✉ 463 rue Sainte-Catherine Ouest ☎ 514/288-9245 🚇 McGill

CLASSICAL MUSIC

ORCHESTRE SYMPHONIQUE DE MONTRÉAL

This world-class orchestra performs most often at the Place des Arts, but also gives summer and Christmas concerts at the Basilique Notre-Dame, and pop classics at the Arena Maurice Richard in the Olympic Park. ☎ 514/842-9951

ORCHESTRE MÉTROPOLITAIN DE MONTRÉAL

Frequent concerts at the Place des Arts. ☎ 514/598-0870

SOCIÉTÉ DE MUSIQUE CONTEMPORAINE DE QUÉBEC (SMCQ)

A well-established, modern classical ensemble.
☎ 514/843-9305

I MUSICI

A much-lauded chamber ensemble.
☎ 514/982-6037

LE STUDIO DE MUSIQUE ANCIENNE

An early music society.
☎ 514/861-2626

MCGILL CHAMBER ORCHESTRA

Performs at the Place des Arts and another key classical venue, the Pollack Hall.
✚ F7 ✉ 555 rue Sherbrooke Ouest ☎ 514/398-4535
Ⓜ McGill

DANCE

Montréal's dance troupes perform at the Place des Arts and neighbourhood cultural centres (Maisons de Culture).
❓ See press (▶ 81) for details

BALLETS CLASSIQUES DE MONTRÉAL

The city's most-famous traditional ballet company, established in 1964.
☎ 514/866-1771

LES GRANDS BALLETS CANADIENS

Québec's leading traditional ballet troupe.
☎ 514/849-8681

LALALA HUMAN STEPS

An acclaimed avant-garde dance company.
☎ 514/277-9090

LES BALLETS JAZZ DE MONTRÉAL

A well-regarded modern dance troupe.
☎ 514/982-6771

FESTIVAL INTERNATIONAL DE NOUVELLE DANSE

For two weeks in late September and early October of odd-numbered years, the city hosts this ever popular modern dance festival.
☎ 514/287-1423

OPERA

L'OPÉRA DE MONTRÉAL

Founded in 1979, the city's opera company stages four productions every year at the Place des Arts.
☎ 514/985-2258

THEATRE

THÉÂTRE DU RIDEAU VERT

One of the best-known of the French-language theatres in Montréal.
✚ D4 ✉ 4664 rue Saint-Denis
☎ 514/844-1793 Ⓜ Laurier

CENTAUR THEATRE

The city's foremost English-language theatre.
✚ G7 ✉ 453 rue Saint-François-Xavier
☎ 514/288-3161 Ⓜ Place d'Armes

COMEDY

COMEDY NEST

Venue for local and visiting comics.
✚ E97 ✉ 4020 rue Sainte-Catherine Ouest
☎ 514/932-6378 Ⓜ Atwater

PLACE DES ARTS

Montréal's showcase for the performing arts has five major performance spaces including the 2,982-seat Salle Wilfrid-Pelletier concert hall. The Place des Arts houses the Orchestre Symphonique de Montréal, the Opéra de Montréal, and the city's principal ballet troupe, Les Grands Ballets Canadiens. Chamber music, plays, other concerts, and an informal Sunday-morning breakfast concert series known as Sons et Brioches are also held here.
✚ F7 ✉ 260 boulevard de Maisonneuve Ouest
☎ Information 514/285-4200; tickets 514/842-2112
🕐 Box office Mon–Fri 10–6
Ⓜ Place-des-Arts

Live Music Venues

MORE LIVE MUSIC

Salsathèque (► 81) has pulsating Latin rhythms with dancing to match; and Pub le Vieux Dublin (► 80) offers live Celtic music that strikes a chord with visitors and Montréalers alike.

L'AIR DU TEMPS

Small, smokey, and intimate, this archetypal jazz club with a great old-fashioned interior lies at the heart of Vieux-Montréal. Come early for a decent seat.

✚ G8 ✉ 191 rue Saint-Paul Ouest ☎ 514/842-2003 ⏰ Live music Wed–Sun 8.30PM–3AM Ⓜ Square-Victoria 💲 Cover charge

BIDDLES

Jazz musician Charlie Biddles is the heart and soul of this downtown local. You can also get some pretty fine chicken and ribs here.

✚ F7 ✉ 2060 rue Aylmer near rue de Maisonneuve Ouest ☎ 514/842-8656 ⏰ Mon–Fri 11AM–2AM; Sat 6.30PM–2AM; Sun 6.30PM–12.30AM. Live jazz every night Ⓜ McGill 💲 Cover charge on weekends and for major acts ❓ Reservations recommended

LE CLUB SODA

Hosts live music plus stand-up comedy and other shows. It buzzes during the Jazz and Juste Pour Rire festivals.

✚ F6 ✉ 1225 boulevard Saint-Laurent ☎ 514/286-1010; www.clubsoda.ca ⏰ 8PM–2AM Ⓜ Saint-Laurent

LES DEUX PIERROTS

A crowded and convivial Vieux-Montréal venue devoted to traditional Québécois folk music. Performances are on the terrace when the weather warms up.

✚ G7 ✉ 104 rue Saint-Paul Est ☎ 514/861-1270 ⏰ Mon–Fri 9AM–6PM Ⓜ Place-d'Armes

HURLEY'S IRISH PUB

Montréal's Celtic music craze started in this comfortable two-floor downtown club—and it is still favourite with the city's Irish community.

✚ E8 ✉ 1225 rue Crescent ☎ 514/861-4111 ⏰ Daily 11AM–3AM Ⓜ Peel, Guy-Concordia

JELLO

American film actors Bruce Willis and Nicholas Cage are among those who have dropped into this 1960s style lounge-club to pick one of the 50 martinis on the drinks list. Live music nearly every night. Ultracomfortable sofas and pool tables.

✚ F6 ✉ 151 rue Ontario Est ☎ 514/285-2621 ⏰ Tue–Fri 5PM–3AM; Sat 9PM–3AM Ⓜ Saint-Laurent

QUAI DES BRUMES

Two quite different jazz bars share a building on rue Saint-Denis (albeit with separate entrances). Downstairs is the calm and intimate Quai des Brumes. Upstairs is the bigger and louder Le Central, which draws a college-age crowd.

✚ E5 ✉ 4479 rue Saint-Denis ☎ 514/845-9010 ⏰ Daily 3PM–3AM Ⓜ Mont-Royal

UPSTAIRS JAZZ CLUB

Local and visiting jazz artists make this a delightful place to pause for a drink or even a meal.

✚ E8 ✉ 1254 rue Mackay ☎ 514/931-6808 ⏰ Mon–Thu noon–1AM; Fri noon–3AM; Sat 5PM–3AM; Sun 5PM–1AM Ⓜ Mont-Royal

Sports

BASEBALL
The Expos play in the Olympic Stadium from April to September.

☩ G1 ✉ Stade Olympique, 4549 avenue Pierre-de-Coubertin ☎ Information 514/253-3434; tickets 514/846-3976 🚇 Viau

CYCLING
Montréal has over 20 specialized cycle paths. Rent bicycles from:

Vélo Aventure
✉ Quai de Convoyeurs
☎ 514/847-0666
Accès Oble
✉ Place Jacques-Cartier
☎ 514/525-8888
Bicycletterie J. R.
✉ 151 rue Rachel Est
☎ 514/843-6989

GOLF
Golf Le Village
☩ G1 ✉ Rue Sherbrooke at rue Viau ☎ 514/872-4653 🚇 Viau **Club de Golf Deux-Montagnes**
This championship course offers 36 holes in a beautiful, lakeside setting.
☩ Off map at A13
☎ 450/472-4653
Club de Gold Mont-Gabriel
This scenic course is an hour's drive from Montréal in the Laurentians.
☩ Off map at A13
☎ 800/668-5253

FOOTBALL
The Alouettes of the professional Canadian Football League play at the open-air Molson Stadium on the McGill University campus.
☩ E7 ☎ 514/872-2266

HOCKEY
Montréal's much-loved hockey team, Les Canadiens, plays at the Molson Centre from October to mid-June.
☩ F8 ✉ Molson Centre, 1260 rue de la Gauchetière Ouest 🚇 Bonaventure

JOGGING
Parc Angrignon (▶ 58) offers gentle, scenic cinder trails or puff up Mont-Royal (▶ 30) on trails of varying steepness.

MOTOR RACING
The Formula One Grand Prix takes place every June on the Île Notre-Dame.
☩ J5–K8 ✉ Circuit Gilles-Villeneuve ☎ 514/871-1421 🚇 Île Sainte-Hélène

SQUASH
Reserve court time at the Nautilus Centre Saint-Laurent Côte-de-Liesse Racquet Club.
☩ Off map at A8 ✉ 8305 chemin Côte-de-Liesse
☎ 514/739-3654 🚇 Du Collège

SWIMMING
Olympic Park has six Olympic-size pools.
☩ G1 ✉ Parc olympique, 4141 avenue Pierre-de-Coubertin ☎ 514/252-4622 or 514/252-8687 🚇 Viau
There are three outdoor pools on the Île Sainte-Hélène and a beach on the Île Notre-Dame.
☩ H4–K8 ☎ 514/872-6211 🚇 Île Ste-Hélène.

WINDSURFING AND SAILING
Small boats and boards can be hired from:
Société de l'Île Notre-Dame
✉ Île Notre-Dame
☎ 514/872-6903
L'École de Voile de Lachine
✉ 2015 boulevard Saint-Joseph, Lachine ☎ 634-4326

CITY PASSION
The Canadiens team has won the National Hockey League's championship Stanley Cup a record 24 times since 1929, which is why they are sometimes called Les Glorieux. No city in Canada is more passionate about Canada's unofficial national sport than Montréal and no uniform is more familiar to hockey fans than the red and white jersey of the Montréal Canadiens with its famous but obscure CH motif. There was a myth the letters stood for Habitants Canadiens, which is why the club is sometimes referred to affectionately as "the Hab," but the letters, in fact, stand for Club de Hockey Canadien.

Luxury Hotels

PRICES AND LOCATION

Expect to pay at least $250 for a double room in a luxury hotel. Most of the big luxury hotels are in downtown, but a new crop of smaller boutique hotels in the luxury and mid-range categories ($130–$250 per nignt) have begun opening in Vieux-Montréal. The trend started in the early 1990s, when there were no hotel rooms in the old city, and continues with new establishments opening virtually every year. Budget accommodations ($85–$130 per night) can be found in the downtown area—notably at the Auberge de Jeunesse (youth hostel) and the YWCA—but most are clustered around the bus terminal and the rue Saint-Denis area. Hotels in all price ranges offer cheaper rates in the low season and many of the business-oriented hotels offer special weekend deals. Some hotels also have family-plan deals that allow children sharing a room with their parents to stay (and sometimes eat) free. Most have rooms equipped with two double beds and some provide a third, smaller bed in the same room for a modest fee.

BONAVENTURE HILTON INTERNATIONAL

Astride the downtown Bonaventure exhibition centre, this 397-room, luxury hotel has an all-season outdoor pool and extensive rooftop gardens.
🚹 F8 ✉ 1 place Bonaventure ☎ 514/878-2332 or toll-free 800/445-8667 in Canada, 800/HILTONS in the US; www.hilton.com 🚇 Bonaventure

CENTRE SHERATON

The huge lobby of this 825-room, business and convention hotel is full of greenery.
🚹 F7 ✉ 1201 boulevard René-Lévesque Ouest ☎ 514/878-2000; www.sheraton.com/lecentre 🚇 Bonaventure or Peel

CHÂTEAU VERSAILLES

This has become one of the city's most elegant hotels with 65 rooms and suites. Many rooms have fireplaces.
🚹 E8 ✉ 1659 rue Sherbrooke Ouest ☎ 514/933-3611 or 888/933-8111 (Canada/US); www.versailleshotels.com 🚇 Guy-Concordia

HÔTEL LE GERMAIN

Ultrachic boutique hotel close to museums and downtown.
🚹 E7 ✉ 2050 rue Mansfield ☎ 514/849–2050 or 877/333-2050; www.hotelboutique.com 🚇 McGill

HÔTEL INTERCONTINENTAL MONTRÉAL

Near to Vieux-Montréal and to the convention centre, this luxury hotel has 357 rooms, a health club, and a swimming pool.
🚹 F7 ✉ 360 rue Saint-Antoine Ouest ☎ 514/987-9900 or toll-free 800/361-3600; www.intercontinental.com 🚇 Square-Victoria

LOEWS HÔTEL VOGUE

Bathrooms in the 154 rooms of this fashionable downtown hotel all have whirlpool baths, televisions, and phones.
🚹 E8 ✉ 1425 rue de la Montague ☎ 514/285-5555 or 800/465-6654; www.loewshotel.com 🚇 Peel/Guy-Concordia

OMNI MONTRÉAL

Excellent service and 300 fine rooms, many with views of Mont-Royal, distinguish this downtown hotel.
🚹 E7 ✉ 1050 Sherbrooke Ouest ☎ 514/284-1110 or toll-free 800/843-6664; www.omnihotels.com 🚇 Peel

PIERRE-DU-CALVERT

American revolutionary Benjamin Franklin was once a guest in this 18th-century building in Vieux-Montréal. There are nine sumptuously decorated rooms. Fine restaurant.
🚹 G8 ✉ 405 rue Bonsecours ☎ 514/282-1725; www.pierreducalvert.com 🚇 Champ-de-Mars

RITZ CARLTON MONTRÉAL

Richard Burton and Liz Taylor held their second marriage at this stately and fashionable Edwardian hotel, with 229 rooms.
🚹 E7 ✉ 1228 rue Sherbrooke Ouest ☎ 514/842-4212; www.ritzcarlton.com 🚇 Peel

Mid-Range Hotels

AUBERGE BONAPARTE

This delightful 31-room inn in the heart of Vieux-Montréal has views of the Basilique Notre-Dame gardens next door.

➕ G7 ✉️ 447 rue Saint-Françoise-Xavier
☎️ 514/844-1448;
www.bonaparte.inc
Ⓜ️ Place d'Armes

AUBERGE DE LA FONTAINE

Intimate hotel near bicycle path faces Parc Lafontaine in the trendy Plateau Mont-Royal district.

➕ F4 ✉️ 1301 rue Rachel Est
☎️ 514/597-0166 or toll-free 800/597-0597;
www.aubergedelafontaine.com
Ⓜ️ Mont-Royal

AUBERGE DU VIEUX-PORT

The 27 pleasant rooms, with brass beds and casement windows, overlook rue Saint-Paul or the Vieux-Port.

➕ G7 ✉️ 97 rue de la Commune Est ☎️ 514/876-0081;
www.aubergeduvieuxport.com
Ⓜ️ Champs-de-Mars

BEST WESTERN EUROPA CENTRE-VILLE

The excellent downtown location and good selection of restaurants here distinguish this 184-room hotel.

➕ E8 ✉️ 1240 rue Drummond
☎️ 514/866-6492 or toll-free 800/361-3000;
www.europahotelmtl.com
Ⓜ️ Peel or Guy-Concordia

HÔTEL DE L'INSTITUT

Top civil servants love this 42-room hotel on the top floors of Québec's best hotel training school, right in the Quartier-Latin.

➕ F6 ✉️ 3535 rue Saint-Denis
☎️ 514/282-5120 or 800/361-5111;
www.hotel.ithq.qc.ca
Ⓜ️ Sherbrooke

HÔTEL DE LA MONTAGNE

There are 138 spacious rooms, a good restaurant, a rooftop terrace, and a pool.

➕ E8 ✉️ 1430 rue de la Montagne ☎️ 514/288-5656 or toll-free 800/361-6262;
www.hoteldelamontagne.com
Ⓜ️ Peel

LE NOUVEL HÔTEL

Modern, functional hotel with 165 rooms in a convenient location.

➕ E8 ✉️ 1740 boulevard René-Lévesque Ouest
☎️ 514/931-8841 or toll-free 800/363-6063;
www.lenouvelhotel.com
Ⓜ️ Guy-Concordia

LES PASSANTS DU SANS SOUCY

The entrance to this charming inn with nine rooms is a functioning art gallery.

➕ G7 ✉️ 171 rue Saint-Paul Ouest ☎️ 514/842-2634;
www.lesanssoucy.com
Ⓜ️ Square-Victoria, Place d'Armes

HÔTEL PLACE D'ARMES

Occupying a beautiful old building, many of the 44 elegantly furnished rooms here have ornate carvings.

➕ G7 ✉️ 701 Place d'Armes
☎️ 514/842-1887 or 888/450-1887;
www.hotelplacedarmes.com
Ⓜ️ Place d'Armes

RESERVATIONS

Although greater Montréal has some 23,000 hotel beds, advance reservations are advisable, particularly from May to August. Even if you guarantee your booking with a credit card, reconfirm a few days ahead. Receptionists are usually bilingual in French and English. If you arrive without accommodation, the city's tourist offices will help you to find a room (► 90).

Budget Accommodation

BED AND BREAKFAST

Bed and breakfast options (*couette et café* in French) can be booked through tourist offices and through the following agencies:

Bed & Breakfast Downtown Network

✉ 3458 avenue Laval
☎ 514/289-9749 or toll-free 800/267-5180

Bed & Breakfast à Montréal Network

✉ 2033 rue Saint-Herbert
☎ 514/738-9410 or toll-free 800/738-4338;
www.bbmontreal.com

Chambre et petit déjeuners Bienvenue

✉ 3950 avenue Laval
☎ 514/844-5897 or toll-free 800/227-5897;
www.bienvenubb.com

AUBERGE DE JEUNESSE YOUTH HOSTEL

Superior hostel with 15 private rooms and 243 dormitory-style beds. Near the Centre Molson and nightlife.

➕ E8 ✉ 1030 rue Mercy
☎ 514/843-3317 or 800/663-3317;
www.hostellingmontreal.com
Ⓜ Lucien l'Allier

HÔTEL LORD BERRI

Good modern hotel with 154 rooms near the bus terminal, the Université du Québec à Montréal, and rue Saint-Denis.

➕ G6 ✉ 1199 rue Berri
☎ 514/845-9236 or toll-free 800/363-0363;
www.lordberri.com
Ⓜ Berri-UQAM

HÔTEL MANOIR SHERBROOKE

Converted Victorian building with 22 pleasant rooms. Rate includes continental breakfast.

➕ F6 ✉ 157 rue Sherbrooke Est ☎ 514/845-0915 or toll-free 800/203-5485;
www.armormanoir.com
Ⓜ Sherbrooke

HÔTEL MARITIME PLAZA

A favourite with visiting bus tours, this hotel has 241 rooms and suites and is convenient for shopping and museums.

➕ E8 ✉ 1155 rue Guy
☎ 514/932-1411 or 800/363-6255 Ⓜ Guy Concord or Lucien L'Allier

QUALITY HOTEL DOWNTOWN

This 140-room hotel's location close to McGill University makes it popular with visiting students and parents.

➕ F7 ✉ 3440 avenue du Parc Avenue ☎ 514/849-1413 or 800/228-5151;
www.choicehotels/cn329
Ⓜ Palce-des-Arts

LA RÉSIDENCE DU VOYAGEUR

Close to the attractions of the Quartier Latin and the Plateau Mont-Royal, this hotel has 28 comfortable rooms. Breakfast is included in the room rate.

➕ F5 ✉ 847 rue Sherbrooke Est ☎ 514/527-9515;
www.hotelresidencevoyager.com
Ⓜ Sherbrooke

HÔTEL LE ROBERVAL

This is a no frills hotel with 43 rooms and suites near to downtown.

➕ G6 ✉ 505 bouevard René-Lévesque Est
☎ 514/286-5215;
www.hotel-roberval.qc.ca
Ⓜ Champ-de-Mars

HÔTEL LE ST-ANDRÉ

Charming 62-room hotel close to Vieux-Montréal and the Quartier Latin.

➕ G6 ✉ 1285 rue Saint-André ☎ 514/849-7070 or toll-free 800/265-7071 in Canada and the US;
www.lesaintandre.montrealplus.ca
Ⓜ Berri-UQAM

YWCA

Fifty simple rooms for single, double, and multiple occupancy. Women guests have access to YWCA health facilities.

➕ E8 ✉ 1355 boulevard René-Lévesque Quest
☎ 514/866-9941 ext. 505;
www.ydesfemmesmtl.org
Ⓜ Lucien L'Allier

MONTRÉAL
travel facts

ESSENTIAL FACTS

Car rental

To rent a car in Montréal you must be 25 or over (21 if using a major credit card).

- Avis ✉ 1225 rue Metcalfe ☎ 514/866–7906 or 800/321-3652.
- Budget ✉ Gare Centrale, 895 rue de la Gauchetière Ouest ☎ 514/866-7675, 938-1000 or 800/268-8970.
- Hertz Canada ✉ 1475 rue Aylmer ☎ 514/842-8537 or 800/263-0678.
- Thrifty-Québec ✉ 1600 rue Berri, Bureau 9 ☎ 514/845-5954 or 800/367-2277
- National ✉ 1200 rue Stanley ☎ 514/878-2771 or 800/387-4747.

Electricity

- Current in Canada is 100 volts AC (60Hz). Plug adaptors are needed for British or European appliances to match the two-prong sockets.

Opening hours

- Shops: Mon–Fri 9 or 9.30–6; Sat 9–5. Some shops open Sun 12–5. Some stores open longer hours Mon–Fri 10–9; Sat 10–6; Sun 12–5.
- Banks: Mon–Fri 9–4. Some larger banks open Sat morning.
- Post offices: Mon–Fri 8.30–5.30. Some open Sat mornings.

Public holidays

- 1 January; Good Friday; Easter Monday; Victoria Day (Monday in mid-May); Fête Nationale (24 June); Canada Day (1 July); Labor Day; Thanksgiving; Remembrance Day; 25 December; 26 December.

Sales tax

- You can reclaim GST (Goods and Services Tax) on accommodation and for goods taken out of the country (purchases of $100 and over).
- Keep receipts and complete the Goods and Services Tax Refund for Visitors form, available from retailers, duty free shops, or Revenue Canada ✉ Visitors' Rebate Program, Ottawa, Ontario K1A 1JS.
- You can apply for a TVQ (Québec Sales Tax) rebate (for goods and services) on the same form.

Tourist information

- Montréal's main tourist office is the Centre Infotouriste ✉ 1001 Square-Dorchester ☎ 514/873-2015 or toll-free 800/363-7777 in Canada and the US ⏰ 1 Jun–Labor Day: daily 8.30– 7.30. Labor Day–31 May: daily 9–5 Ⓜ Peel.
  There is a smaller tourist information office in Vieux-Montréal ✉ 174 rue Notre-Dame Est at Place Jacques-Cartier ☎ 514/873-2015 ⏰ Mid-May to Labor Day: daily 9–7. Labor Day to mid-May: daily 9–1, 2–5.
  Information kiosks at the Aéroport de Mirabel ⏰ Daily 12–2.30, 3–8 and Aéroport de Dorval ⏰ Daily 1–8.

Women travellers

- Montréal's streets are considerably safer than those of most North-American cities. However, parks, back streets, and unlit areas should be avoided after dark.

PUBLIC TRANSPORTATION

Routes and tickets

- Contact STCUM (Société de Transport de la Communauté Urbaine de Montréal) ☎ 514/288-6287 or 514/280-5666 ⏰ Mon–Fri 7AM–11PM; Sat, Sun, public hols 8AM–10PM.

Métro and bus services

- Four key stations provide the main interchanges between lines: Berri-UQAM (orange, green, and yellow lines); Lionel Groulx (green and orange); Snowdon (blue and orange); Jean-Talon (blue and orange).
- A one-day or three-day tourist pass—*Carte touristique* (Tourist Card)—allows you to travel at will on buses or Métro. Both may be purchased from the tourist office or downtown hotels.
- A transfer system allows you to complete a Métro journey by bus (and vice versa) at no extra cost. A transfer ticket (*correspondance*) is available from machines in the Métro, and valid for one hour. Bus-to-bus or bus-to-Métro transfers can be obtained from drivers as you board a bus. However, Métro transfers cannot be used to gain re-entry to the Métro.
- The STCUM also operates two commuter train lines. One, leaving from Gare Windsor and the Vendôme Métro station, runs as far west as Hudson and Regaud. The other runs north from Gare Centrale to Deux-Montagnes. Weekend service is sparse. Tickets are available from machines at stations, but all STCUM passes are good for travel within Zone 1 on both lines. Fares depend on distance.

Taxis

Cab companies include:
- Co-op ☎ 725-9885
- Diamond ☎ 273-6331
- La Salle ☎ 277-2552

A 10–15 percent tip is normal.

MEDIA & COMMUNICATIONS

Mail

- Montréal's main post office is Postes Canada ✚ F8 ✉ 1025 rue Saint-Jacques near rue de la Cathédrale ☎ 514/283-2567 🚇 Bonaventure.
- Smaller post offices can be found inside shops, department stores, and train stations wherever there are Postes Canada signs.
- Stamps can be bought from post offices, the Centre Infotouriste in Square-Dorchester (► 90), train station and bus terminals, and airports, in addition to convenience stores.
- Within Canada, postcards and letters up to 30g are 48¢; up to 100g, 98¢; and 200–500g, $2.10. Cards and letters to the US cost 65¢ up to 30g. Rates for other destinations are $1.25 up to 30g and $1.75 from 30 to 50g.
- Letters sent *poste restante* should be sent to the main post office marked "c/o General Delivery" or "c/o Poste Restante." State a collection date if possible, otherwise letters will be returned to the sender after 15 days. Take photo identification (e.g. passport, driver's licence) when collecting mail. Letters sent for collection in hotels should be marked "Guest Mail, Hold for Arrival."
- Telepost is a 24-hour, seven-days-a-week service whereby messages can be phoned to the nearest CN/CP Communications Public Message Centre (details from hotels or tourist offices) for a telegram-like delivery anywhere in Canada or the US the next day or sooner.

Newspapers, television & radio

- Canada has two national newspapers—*The Globe* and the *Mail and the National Post*. The English-language daily is *The Montréal Gazette*. French dailies are *La Presse* and the tabloid *Journal de Montréal*. *Voire* and *Heure* are French-speaking alternate weeklies that have details of what's on in the city; *Hour* and *Mirror* are the English equivalents. Major American papers are available on the day of publication.
- Canada has three national television networks: the Canadian Broadcasting Corporation (CBC), CTV, and Global. Most American networks are also available
- CBC Radio 1 at 88.5MHz offers news and public-affairs programming; Radio 2 serves classical music and cultural programming at 93.5MHz. The best English station for local news, talk, and traffic reports is CJAD at 800kHz and the best French one is CKAC at 730kHz.

Telephones

- Local calls from phone booths cost 25¢. This includes calls to all numbers in the 514 area code—all municipalities on the island of Montréal itself— and to some numbers in the surrounding 450 area code (in such off-island suburbs as Laval, Longueuil, and Brossard). The rest of the 450 area code and all other area codes are long distance and you will need to dial 1 to get an operator to tell you how much money you need to make the connection. Thereafter, have plenty of 25¢ pieces on hand to continue the call. If you're calling a 450 number and you're not sure whether it is local or long distance, try dialing 1 before the number: You will either get through or you will get a recording telling you it is a local call.
- For a number outside the area you are in, including all toll-free numbers, dial 1, then the area code, followed by 555-1212.
- For international and long-distance calls, buy a Hello! Phone Pass, or find public phones that accept credit cards. At the Bell-Canada office you can phone and pay for your call afterwards ✉ Bureau Public, 700 rue de la Gauchetière Ouest at rue University 🕐 Mon–Fri 9–5.
- Direct dial phones are common in many hotels and motels. A surcharge is levied.
- Many organizations have toll-free numbers—800, 888, or 877 prefix. Some operate within a province, others in Canada, and a few from North America.
- Collect calls can be made by dialing 0 for the operator.
- Information for local numbers can be reached by dialing 411.
- To call the US from Canada dial the area code and the number.
- To call the UK from Canada dial 011 44, followed by the area code (minus its first zero), and the number required.
- To call Canada from the US dial 1, the area code, and then the number .
- To call Canada from the UK dial 001, then the area code (minus its first zero), and then the number.

EMERGENCIES

Emergency telephone numbers

- Police, fire, ambulance ☎ 911 or dial 0 for the operator, who will then connect you to the appropriate service.
- Montréal General Hospital ✉ 1650 Cedar ☎ 514/937-6011 Royal Victoria Hospital ✉ 687 avenue Pine Ouest ☎ 514/842-1231 Montréal Children's Hospital ✉ 2300 rue Tupper ☎ 514/934-4499 or 934-4400.
- Lost property: bus or Métro ☎ 514/280-4637; taxis ☎ 514/280-6660 Elsewhere contact the MUC Police ☎ 514/280-4636.
- Lawyer referrals contact the Québec Bar Association ☎ 514/954-3413.
- US Consulate ✉ 1155 rue Saint-Alexandre ☎ 514/398-9695 US Embassy ✉ 490 Sussex Drive, Ottawa ☎ 613/238-5335.
- UK Consulate ✉ 1155 rue University ☎ 514/866-5863 🚇 McGill.
- British Embassy ✉ 80 Elgin Street, Ottawa ☎ 613/237-1530.
- Irish Embassy ✉ 130 Albert Street, Ottawa ☎ 613/233-6281.

Safety Precautions

- By North-American standards, Montréal is remarkably crime free. But it's wise to play safe. Don't leave luggage or valuables in cars, don't carry around large quantities of cash, and keep your passports and credit cards in a pouch or money belt. Avoid parks, the area around the train station, and other noncommercial parts of the city after dark. Leave valuables in a hotel safe—or at home.

Medical and dental treatment

- If you need a doctor, first contact your hotel. Lists of doctors are available from consulates and in the Yellow Pages, otherwise you can try the Information and Referral Centre ☎ 514/527-1375 🕐 Mon–Fri 8.30–4.45. If it is outside office hours, contact the nearest hospital or CLS (Centre local de service communautaires) health clinic.
- For information about dental treatment call the Ordre des dentistes du Québec ☎ 875-8511. There is a 24-hour dental clinic at ✉ 3546 avenue Van Horne ☎ 514/342-4444.
- For information about opticians call the Ordre des Opticiens ☎ 514/288-7542.
- Most over-the-counter medicines can be bought at drug stores. If you need medicine on a prescription there is a 24-hour pharmacy at ✉ 5122 chemin de la Côte-des-Neiges ☎ 514/738-8464. Bring a prescription with you if you need to renew medication. This will avoid problems at customs and help the pharmacist.

Useful telephone numbers

- American Express ☎ 514/284-3300/392-4422; lost or stolen cards ☎ 514/281-9824.
- MasterCard ☎ 514/877-8610 or 800/307-7309.
- Visa ☎ 800/847-2911.
- Road breakdown ☎ 800/CAA-HELP or 514/861-1313.
- Thomas Cook ☎ 514/398-0555 or 514/397-4029.
- Touring Club de Montréal-CAA-AAA-RAC ☎ 514/861-7111.
- Weather ☎ 514/636-3026.

Index

CityPack
Montréal

ABOUT THE AUTHOR

Tim Jepson's love of travel began with a busking trip through Europe and has taken him from the Umbrian countryside to the Canadian Rockies and the windswept tundra of the Yukon. Future plans include walking the length of Italy and exploring the Arctic and South America. Tim has written several books for the AA, including *Explorer* guides to Canada, Rome, Italy, Florence & Tuscany, and Venice. Other publications include *Rough Guides* to Canada and The Pacific Northwest.

EDITION REVISER	Paul Waters
MAPS	© Automobile Association Developments Limited 2003
COVER DESIGN	© Automobile Association Developments Limited 2003

A CIP catalogue record for this book is available from the British Library.

ISBN 0 7495 3582 2

All rights reserved. No part of this publication may be reproduced, stored in a retrieval system or transmitted in any form or by any means—electronic, photocopying, recording or otherwise—unless the written permission of the publishers has been obtained beforehand. This book may not be lent, resold, hired out or otherwise disposed of by way of trade in any form of binding or cover other than that in which it is published, without the prior consent of the publishers.

The contents of this publication are believed correct at the time of printing. Nevertheless, the publishers cannot be held responsible for any errors or omissions or for changes in the details given in this guide or for the consequences of any reliance on the information provided by the same. This does not affect your statutory rights. Assessments of attractions, hotels, restaurants, and so forth are based upon the author's own personal experience and, therefore, descriptions given in this guide necessarily contain an element of subjective opinion which may not reflect the publishers' opinion or dictate a reader's own experiences on another occasion. We have tried to ensure accuracy in this guide, but things do change and we would be grateful if readers would advise us of any inaccuracies they may encounter.

Published by AA Publishing, a trading name of Automobile Association Developments Limited, whose registered office is Millstream, Maidenhead Road, Windsor, Berkshire, SL4 5GD. Registered number 1878835.

© **AUTOMOBILE ASSOCIATION DEVELOPMENTS LIMITED 1997, 2000, 2003**
First published 1997. Second edition 2000. Third edition 2003.

Colour separation by Daylight Colour Art Pte Ltd., Singapore
Printed and bound by Dai Nippon Printing Co. (Hong Kong) Ltd.

ACKNOWLEDGEMENTS
The Automobile Association would like to thank the following photographers, libraries and associations for their assistance in their preparation of this book:
BIODÔME DE MONTRÉAL 37; CENTRE CANADIEN D'ARCHITECTURE 32; CENTRE D'HISTORIE DE MONTRÉAL 39b; HULTONARCHIVE 17l, 17r; IMAGOS (C. Coe) 45b; MARY EVANS PICTURES LIBRARY 16l, 16c, 16r; MRI BANKERS GUIDE TO FOREIGN CURRENCY 6; MUSÉE DES BEAUX-ARTS DE MONTRÉAL 31b; STOCKBYTE 5; TOURISME MONTRÉAL 1t, 2, 4, 6tl (Anton's Photo Express), 13t (Canadian Tourism Commission, Pierre St-Jaques), 24cl (Casino de Montréal), 15cr (Cöpilia), 9cr (Daniel Choinière), 14/15 (Just for Laughs Festival, Gilles Menon), 8bt (Just for Laughs Festival, Martin Savard), 12c (Montréal Biodôme, Sean O'Neill), 11c, 15c (Montréal Botanical Garden), 14tr (Musée d'art contemporain de Montréal, Richard-Marx Tremblay), 24cr (Old Port of Montréal Corporation Inc., APES), 8br, 11t, 11ct (Parc Jean-Drapeau, Bernard Brault), 9rb (Parc Jean-Drapeau, Bob Burch), 1b, 8r, 8/9, 9t, 10c, 10r, 12tl, 12tr, 14tl, 15cl, 15t, 16t, 18t, 18l, 18r, 19l, 19r, 20t (Stéphan Poulin), 10/11 (Michel Tremblay), 13c (Windsor Station, Canadian Pacific Railway) 13c. The remaining pictures are held in the Assocation's own library (AA PHOTO LIBRARY) and were taken by JEAN-FRANÇOIS PIN.

A01084
Fold out map © Mairs Geographischer Verlag / Falk Verlag, 73751 Ostfildern
Transport map © TCS, Aldershot, England

TITLES IN THE CITYPACK SERIES